Managing Risk and Information Security

Protect to Enable

Malcolm Harkins

Managing Risk and Information Security: Protect to Enable

Malcolm Harkins

ISBN-13 (pbk): 978-1-4302-5113-2

ISBN-13 (electronic): 978-1-4302-5114-9

Trademarked names, logos, and images may appear in this book. Rather than use a trademark symbol with every occurrence of a trademarked name, logo, or image we use the names, logos, and images only in an editorial fashion and to the benefit of the trademark owner, with no intention of infringement of the trademark.

The use in this publication of trade names, trademarks, service marks, and similar terms, even if they are not identified as such, is not to be taken as an expression of opinion as to whether or not they are subject to proprietary rights.

President and Publisher: Paul Manning
Lead Editors: Jeffrey Pepper (Apress); Stuart Douglas (Intel)
Coordinating Editor: Jill Balzano
Cover Designer: Anna Ishchenko

Distributed to the book trade worldwide by Springer Science+Business Media New York, 233 Spring Street, 6th Floor, New York, NY 10013. Phone 1-800-SPRINGER, fax (201) 348-4505, e-mail orders-ny@springer-sbm.com, or visit www.springeronline.com.

For information on translations, please e-mail rights@apress.com, or visit www.apress.com.

About ApressOpen

What Is ApressOpen?

- ApressOpen is an open access book program that publishes high-quality technical and business information.

- ApressOpen eBooks are available for global, free, noncommercial use.

- ApressOpen eBooks are available in PDF, ePub, and Mobi formats.

- The user friendly ApressOpen free eBook license is presented on the copyright page of this book.

Foreword

Newly promoted CISOs rapidly realize that the scope of the position they have taken on is often beyond what they have been prepared for. The nature of securing an enterprise is daunting and overwhelming. There are no simple checklists or roadmaps for success. Many of the technical security skills a CISO has acquired during the early portion of his or her career may provide a "sixth sense" or intuition, but technical expertise alone does not prepare the CISO for the business and leadership challenges required for success.

The Dunning-Kruger effect "is a cognitive bias in which unskilled individuals suffer from illusory superiority, mistakenly rating their ability much higher than average" (Wikipedia). Successful CISOs generally realize and admit to themselves how much they don't know. In my career, I have met many senior security professionals and have noticed a common set of traits among those who are successful.

They generally exhibit a strong sense of curiosity, the ability to be self-aware, the ability to "think evil" (like the adversary), and have strong communication and critical thinking skills. They are open to new ideas, they invite debate, and they are adaptive in their thinking and positions when new information is presented. They develop leadership skills and build structures that enable balance. They also recognize talent and surround themselves with teams of capable security technologists who are the true experts. Excellent security leaders have learned that risk is not black-and-white and that balance needs to be applied. They are empathic and likeable. My friend Malcolm meets all these criteria.

In *Managing Risk and Information Security: Protect to Enable*, he distills the hard-acquired knowledge he has learned through his career as a business and security leader into a concise framework that enables CISOs to cut through the chaos of securing the enterprise. Absorb the lessons in this book and enrich them by continuing to experiment and innovate. Threats, organizational dynamics, and technology are constantly evolving and we as security professionals must apply the lessons outlined here and continuously adapt ourselves to the challenge.

—Patrick Heim
Chief Trust Officer
Salesforce.com, Inc.

Contents at a Glance

Contents

About the Author

Malcolm Harkins is vice president of the Information Technology Group, Chief Information Security Officer (CISO) and general manager of Information Risk and Security. The group is responsible for managing the risk, controls, privacy, security, and other related compliance activities for all of Intel's information assets.

Before becoming Intel's first CISO, Harkins held roles in Finance, Procurement, and Operations. He has managed IT benchmarking efforts and Sarbanes-Oxley systems compliance efforts. Before moving into IT, Harkins acted as the profit-and-loss manager for the Flash Product Group at Intel; he was the general manager of Enterprise Capabilities, responsible for the delivery and support of Intel's Finance and HR systems; and he worked in an Intel business venture focusing on e-commerce hosting.

Harkins previously taught at the CIO Institute at the UCLA Anderson School of Business and he was an adjunct faculty member at Susquehanna University in 2009. In 2010, he received the award for excellence in the field of security at the RSA Conference. He was recognized by *Computerworld* magazine as one of the top 100 Information Technology Leaders for 2012. In addition, (ISC)2 recognized Malcolm in 2012 with the Information Security Leadership Award.

Harkins received his bachelor's degree in economics from the University of California at Irvine and an MBA in finance and accounting from the University of California at Davis.

Preface

Many organizations failed to survive the information technology revolution. Many more will not survive the current wave of technology-driven innovation—and the threats and vulnerabilities that come with it.

To thrive in complex, highly-connected global markets, organizations need bold business strategies that use technology to achieve competitive advantage. The enterprise information risk and security team can either hinder these strategies or help drive them. Effectively managing information risk and security, without hindering the organization's ability to move quickly, will be key to business survival. That is why, three years ago, I changed the mission of Intel's information risk and security team to *"Protect to Enable."* It is also why I am writing this book.

In January of 2002 I was hired to run a program called Security and Business Continuity. This program was created after the events of 9/11 and the Code Red/Nimda viruses during the summer of 2001. It was primarily focused on the availability risk concerns at that time. I had no technical security background but had been with Intel close to 10 years in a variety of business-related positions that were mostly in finance. It became apparent to me in those first few months as I was learning that the world was going to start dramatically changing and a "perfect storm" of risk was beginning to brew. The following picture is what I put together to explain that to my manager, Intel's CIO, and anyone who would listen to me.

In February of 2004, I left this program since we were mostly done with the effort to deal with the availability risks. I left to run our system's Sarbanes-Oxley compliance efforts. My finance background, the variety of business roles I had previously held, and my time being around IT for so many years as well as the effort I had led in 2002 and 2003 made it a natural fit. But I had something else haunting me, which was this picture. I wasn't haunted by the fear of the risks that could occur, but rather it fueled my sense of curiosity and triggered in me a passion to figure out how to navigate this storm of risk. So in 2005, once our initial SOX compliance efforts were complete, I went back to information security but with a drive and desire to try to link all the main elements of information risk, security, control, and compliance activities together to deal with this spiral of risk. So for the past 7 years, this has been my quest. In this book, I will cover many things I have learned in the 11 years that I have been managing various aspects of information risk and security, at Intel. I will share ways to think about risk, ways to look at governance. I will explore internal and external partnerships for information sharing and collaboration that can make a difference. I will share the examples of things we have done within Intel and things we are looking to do to better manage our risks and enable our IT users. Finally, I will look to the future as well as share my perspectives on the skills required for the 21st-century CISO.

Managing Risk and Information Security: Protect to Enable is a journey, but there is no finish line. Our approach to managing information risk must continue to evolve as rapidly as the pace of business and technology change. My hope is that people will read this book and begin their own journey.

Acknowledgments

This book is dedicated to my family: my father, John; my mother, Mary; my children Colin, Evan, and Erin; and the woman who completes me—my wife, Kim.

In developing this book, I received help from many people within Intel Corporation and throughout the industry.

Special thanks to Mike Faden—our discussions, and his questions seeking clarity from me, brought this book to life. Thanks also to Ilene Aginsky, who encouraged me to start the book, and to Elaine Rainbolt, who has provided considerable help along the way.

I also wish to thank all those in Intel's information risk and security team. Without their skills and passion, I would not have learned so much during the past 11 years. It is because of them that I have been able to execute my role and write this book. Many individuals contributed time, energy, and expertise—either to me, helping me grow my knowledge over the years; directly to the book; or to the creation of other documents that I used as source materials. The following deserve special thanks: Brian Willis, Kim Owen, Steve Mancini, Dennis Morgan, Jerzy Rub, Esteban Gutierrez, Rob Evered, Matt Rosenquist, Tim Casey, Toby Kohlenberg, Jeff Boerio, Alan Ross, Tarun Viswanathan, Matt White, Michael Sparks, Eran Birk, Bill Cahill, Stacy Purcell, Tim Verrall, Todd Butler, Stuart Tyler, Amir Itzhaki, Carol Kasten, Perry Olson, Mary Rossell, Marie Steinmetz, Fawn Taylor, Grant Babb, Eamonn Sheeran, and Dave Munsey.

Other experts who have helped me to learn and grow include the members of the Bay Area CSO Council and Executive Security Action Forum, the members and staff of the Information Risk Executive Council, and participants in the Evanta CISO Executive Summits. In particular, I'd like to acknowledge peers who act as trusted sounding boards for ideas, for me and for others in the industry: Patrick Heim, Dave Cullinane, Justin Somani, Gary Terrell, Larry Brock, Mark Weatherford, Brett Whalin, Joshua Davis, Dennis Brixius, Preston Wood, Anne Kuhns, Roland Cloutier, and John Stewart.

Finally, I wish to thank Intel's past CIOs who challenged and inspired me, and took risks by placing me in roles I wasn't ready for: Carlene Ellis, Louis Burns, Doug Busch, John Johnson, and Diane Bryant.

CHAPTER 1

■ ■ ■

Introduction

There are two primary choices in life: to accept conditions as they exist, or accept the responsibility for changing them.

—Denis Waitley

Given that security breaches and intrusions continue to be reported daily across organizations of every size, is information security really effective? Given the rapid evolution of new technologies and uses, does the information security group even need to exist?

Obviously, this is a somewhat rhetorical question. I cannot imagine that any sizeable organization would operate well without an information security function. The real issue is whether the information security group should continue to exist as it does today, with its traditional mission and vision.

As information security professionals, we should be asking ourselves pointed questions if we wish to remain valuable and relevant to our organizations. Why do we exist? What should our role be? How are new consumer technologies shaping what we do—and can we shape the world of the consumer? How is the evolving threat landscape shaping us—and can we shape the threat landscape? Given the bewildering pace at which technology changes and new threats appear, how do we focus and prioritize our workload? What skills do we need?

Traditionally, information security groups within businesses and other organizations have taken a relatively narrow view of security risks, which resulted in a correspondingly narrow charter. We focused on specific types of threats, such as malware. To combat these threats, we applied technical security controls. To prevent attacks from reaching business applications and employees' PCs, we fortified the network perimeter using firewalls and intrusion detection software. To prevent unauthorized entry to data centers, we installed physical access control systems. Overall, our thinking revolved around how to lock down information assets to minimize security risks.

Today, however, I believe that this narrow scope not only fails to reflect the full range of technology-related risk to the business, it may be detrimental to the business overall. Because this limited view misses many of the risks that affect the organization, it leaves areas of risk unmitigated and therefore leaves the organization vulnerable in those areas. It also makes us vulnerable to missing the interplay between risks and controls: By implementing controls to mitigate one risk, we may actually create a different risk.

As I'll explain in this book, we need to shift our primary focus to adopt a broader view of risk that reflects the pervasiveness of technology today. Organizations still need traditional security controls, but they are only part of the picture.

There are several reasons for this. All stem from the reality that technology plays an essential role in most business activities and in people's daily lives.

Technology has become the central nervous system of a business, supporting the flow of information that drives each business process from product development to sales. The role of technology in peoples' personal lives has expanded dramatically, too, and the boundaries between business and personal use of technology are blurring. Marketers want to use social media to reach more consumers. Employees want to use their personal smartphones to access corporate e-mail.

Meanwhile, the regulatory environment is expanding rapidly, affecting the way that information systems must manage personal, financial, and other information in order to comply—and introducing a whole new area of IT-related business risks.

Threats are also evolving quickly, as attackers develop more sophisticated techniques—often targeted at individuals—that can penetrate or bypass controls such as network firewalls.

In combination, these factors create a set of interdependent risks related to IT, as shown in Figure 1-1.

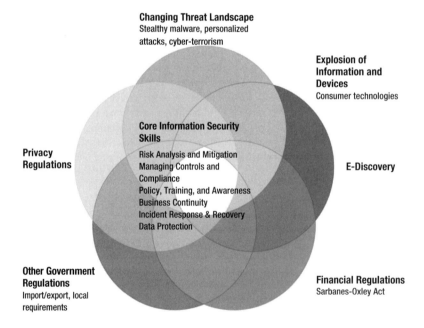

Figure 1-1. *Interdependent risks related to IT. Source: Intel Corporation, 2012*

Traditional security thinkers would respond to this by saying "no" to any technology that introduces new risks. Or perhaps they would allow a new technology but try to heavily restrict it to a narrow segment of the employee population. Marketers should not engage consumers with social media on the company's web site, because this means accumulating personal information that increases the risk of noncompliance with privacy regulations. Employees cannot use personal devices because they are less secure than managed business PCs.

The reality is that because IT is now integrated into everything that an organization does, security groups cannot simply focus on locking down information assets to minimize risk. Restricting the use of information can constrain or even disable the organization, hindering its ability to act and slowing its response to changing market conditions. A narrow focus on minimizing risk therefore introduces a larger danger: it can threaten a business's ability to compete in an increasingly fast-moving environment.

Protect to Enable

To understand how the role of information security needs to change, we need to reexamine our purpose. We need to *Start with Why*, as author Simon Sinek argues convincingly in his book of the same name (Portfolio, 2009). Why does the information security group exist?

As I considered this question and discussed it with other members of Intel's internal information security team, I realized that we needed to redefine our mission. Like the IT organization as a whole, we exist to enable the business—to help deliver IT capabilities that provide competitive differentiation. Rather than focusing primarily on locking down assets, the mission of the information security group must shift to enabling the business while applying a reasonable level of protection. To put it another way, we provide the protection that enables information to flow through the organization.

The core competencies of information security groups—such as risk analysis, business continuity, incident response, and security controls—remain equally relevant as the scope of information-related risk expands to new areas like privacy and financial regulations. But rather than saying "no" to new initiatives, we need to figure out how to say "yes" and think creatively about how to manage the risk.

Within Intel, the role of our security group has evolved toward this goal over the past several years, as we have helped define solutions to a variety of technology challenges.

Starting in 2002, we recognized that implementing wireless networks within Intel's offices could help make our workforce more productive and increase their job satisfaction by letting them more easily connect using their laptops from meeting rooms, cafeterias, and other locations. At the time, many businesses avoided installing wireless networks within their facilities because of the risk of eavesdropping or because of the cost. We learned pretty quickly that when we restricted wireless LAN deployments or charged departments additional fees to connect, we actually generated more risks. This was because the departments would buy their own access points and operate them in an insecure fashion. We recognized that the benefits of installing wireless LANs across the company outweighed the risks, and we mitigated those risks using security controls such as device authentication and transport encryption. Today, our employees see wireless LANs as indispensable business tools.

A more recent example: for years, Intel—like many other organizations—didn't allow employees to use personal smartphones for business, due to privacy concerns and risks such as the potential for data theft. However, we experienced growing demand from employees who owned personal smartphones, and we realized that letting them use these consumer devices to access e-mail and other corporate systems would help boost employee satisfaction and productivity.

By working closely with Intel's legal and human resources (HR) groups, we defined security controls and usage policies that enabled us to begin allowing access to corporate e-mail and calendars from employee-owned smartphones in early 2010. The initiative has been highly successful, with a massive uptake by employees, overwhelmingly positive feedback, and proven productivity benefits (Evered and Rub 2010, Miller and Varga 2011).

The transformation within Intel's information security group is reflected in changes to our mission statement and top priorities over the years, as shown in Figure 1-2. In 2003, our internal mission statement reflected the traditional focus and scope of information security organizations: our overarching goal was to protect Intel's information assets and minimize business disruption.

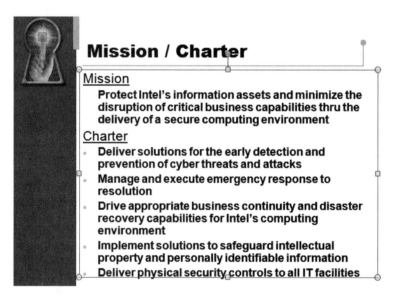

Figure 1-2a. How the mission of Intel's Information Security Group has changed: the mission and priorities in 2003. Source: Intel Corporation, 2012

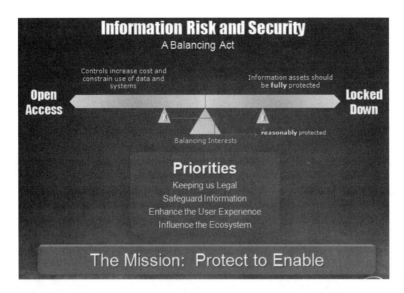

Figure 1-2b. *How the mission of Intel's Information Security Group has changed: the mission and priorities in 2012. Source: Intel Corporation, 2012*

By late 2011, we had changed our mission to Protect to Enable. Our primary goal is now to find ways to enable the business while providing the protection that's necessary to reduce the risk to an acceptable level.

I think of information security as a balancing act. We try to find the right balance between providing open access to technology and information—to enable the business— and locking down assets. Providing open access allows greater business agility. The business can move more quickly with fewer restrictions. Employees can work more freely, and the faster flow of information allows the company to grow and transform.

Within this mission, our priorities reflect the shift in emphasis and our broader view of information risk, as well as the way that the security landscape has changed since 2003.

- *Keeping the company legal.* Compliance, which didn't merit a mention in our 2003 priority list, surged to the top of the list in 2011. This is driven by the growing regulatory environment and the resulting impact on IT.

- *Safeguarding information.* Protecting information assets—our overall mission in 2003—has not disappeared from our list of priorities. However, it has become only one of several items on the list.

- *Enhancing the user experience.* Positioning this as a priority might seem counterintuitive. After all, traditional security groups are better known for blocking users' access. But it's essential to keep the user's experience in mind when devising security policies and controls. If we make it difficult or time-consuming for users to follow security policies, they'll ignore them. In a competitive industry, a delay of

10 minutes can mean losing a sale. When faced with a choice of following policy or losing a customer's business, which do you think a salesperson would choose?

- *Influencing the ecosystem.* In most industries, companies are collaborating more—they are partnering, specializing, and outsourcing. The growing need to exchange information means that compromise to one company can more easily spread to business partners. However, there are also opportunities for businesses to collaborate on security initiatives and standards that help the industry overall; think of the benefits to healthcare companies of being able to securely exchange patient information. Each company benefits by influencing the ecosystem to become more secure.

Though this list represents our current priorities at Intel, I hope that it may be useful for information security groups at other organizations to think about how these priorities relate to their own businesses.

The balancing point between providing open access and locking down assets depends on the organization's appetite for risk. At Intel, informed risk-taking is part of a culture that is designed to help foster innovation. Other businesses may have a different level of risk tolerance.

To analyze the context that has led to our security mission and top priorities, I'll explore some of the key changes in the landscape that affect how we view and manage risk: the rapidly expanding regulatory environment, the emergence of new devices and technologies, and the changing threat landscape.

Keeping the Company Legal: The Regulatory Flood

Until the early 2000s, I didn't see regulatory compliance as a top priority for information security. That's simply because there weren't many regulations that impacted IT, at least in the United States. There were a few exceptions that affected a subset of companies, including Intel, such as controls on certain high-tech exports. And in European countries, there were already regulations that sought to protect personal information. But in general, IT groups didn't have to dedicate much of their time—or budget—to regulatory compliance.

The change in the last decade has been extraordinary. We have seen a flood of new regulations implemented at local, national, and international levels. They affect the storage and protection of information across the entire business, from the use of personal information for HR and marketing purposes, to financial data, to the discovery of almost any type of document or electronic communication in response to lawsuits. And with growing concerns about cyberwarfare, cyberterrorism, and hacktivism, several countries are evaluating additional cybersecurity legislation in an attempt to protect critical infrastructure and make industries more accountable for strengthening security controls.

In most cases, these regulations do not aim to specifically define IT capabilities; however, because information is stored electronically, there are huge implications for IT. The controls defined in the regulations ultimately must be implemented in the organization's systems. These systems include more than just technology: they consist of people, procedures, devices, and applications. The business risk includes a significant IT-related component, but we must take a holistic view of risk management. Noncompliance can damage a company's brand image, profitability, and stock price—not just through resulting legal problems, but through bad publicity.

Let's take a brief look at some of the key areas and regulations that are having the biggest impact.

Privacy: Protecting Personal Information

For many US companies, the wake-up call was the California data security breach notification law (State Bill 1386), which became effective in 2003. A key aspect of this law requires companies that store personal information to notify the owner of the information in the event of a known or suspected security breach. Businesses could reduce their exposure, as well as the risk to individuals, by encrypting personal data.

After this, other states quickly followed suit, implementing regulations that generally follow the basic tenets of California's original law: companies must promptly disclose a data breach to customers, usually in writing.

In addition, federal laws, such as the Health Insurance Portability and Accountability Act (HIPAA), have addressed specific categories of personal information. Further regulations have been added in other countries, too, such as the updated data-protection privacy laws implemented in Europe (European Commission 2011, 2012).

The implications of these local and national regulations extend beyond geographical boundaries. As companies do more business online, they're increasingly likely to acquire and store information about customers from other countries—and find they also need to comply with regulations around the world. For example, citizens of European countries may register on the web site of a US business so that they can receive information and product updates.

The issue becomes even more complex when businesses outsource application development or HR functions to providers located in yet another country. Now, software developers in India may be building and operating the systems that collect information about Europeans for US companies, making it even more difficult for businesses to navigate compliance with all relevant privacy regulations.

Personalization versus Privacy

Privacy concerns are set to become even more important over time, as businesses increasingly seek to create online experiences tailored to the needs of individual users. The more a business knows about each individual, the more it can personalize services and offer targeted advertising based on income and preferences.

Many users also like personalized services. If a web site "remembers" them, they don't need to enter the same information each time they visit the site, and they're more likely to see content and offers relevant to their needs. In fact, companies may be at a disadvantage if they don't personalize services, because users may prefer a web site from a competitor that offers a more streamlined experience.

However, there's an inevitable conflict between personalization and privacy. The personalization trend is fueling the growth of an industry focused on collecting, analyzing, and reselling information about individuals. This industry existed long before the Web; personal information has been used in mass-mailing campaigns for decades. However, the Web is both increasing demand for this information while providing new ways to collect it. Companies now have opportunities to collect information from multiple online sources, correlate and analyze this information, and then sell it to others. And of course, consumers' fears that information will be lost or misused have increased accordingly.

For businesses, however, offering personalized services also can increase compliance concerns. As companies store more personal information, they are responsible for safeguarding that information and are liable for any loss or compromise. In many parts of the world, companies are also required to explain why they are collecting personal data, how they are protecting it, and how long they will keep it.

We can expect continuing tension due to conflicting desires for personalization and privacy—and more regulation as a result. Governments clearly believe that businesses cannot be relied upon to regulate themselves, so they will continue to add regulations designed to protect the privacy of individuals. Meanwhile, businesses will seek new ways to collect more information so that they can further personalize services. Developing compliance strategies and guidelines becomes even more pressing.

Financial Regulations

Financial regulation surfaced as a top priority in the United States with the Sarbanes-Oxley Act (SOX), which emerged from the public outrage over corporate and financial accounting scandals at companies such as Enron and WorldCom. These scandals cost investors billions of dollars and damaged public confidence. To help avoid similar catastrophes in future, SOX imposed financial tracking requirements designed to ensure that a company's financial reporting is accurate and that there hasn't been fraud or manipulation. Once enacted, SOX required publicly held companies to meet specific financial reporting requirements by the end of 2004.

Though the Sarbanes-Oxley Act doesn't mandate specific technology controls, it has major implications for IT. Ensuring financial integrity requires controls to be implemented within everyday financial processes. In practice, this means they must be enforced within the IT applications and infrastructure that support those processes. Purchases above specific thresholds may require approval from the finance group; the underlying applications have to support this workflow, and to be sure the applications function correctly, businesses need to establish the integrity of the underlying computer infrastructure. Compliance with financial regulations therefore creates a series of IT requirements, from making sure that applications provide the right functionality to implementing access controls and updating software. This compliance comes at a steep cost: enterprises surveyed by Gartner, Inc. (2005) estimated that 10 to 15 percent of their entire IT budgets in 2006 would be spent on financial regulatory compliance.

e-Discovery

Regulations governing the discovery of information for litigation purposes officially extended their reach into the electronic realm in 2006. That's when the US Supreme Court's amendments to the Federal Rules of Civil Procedure explicitly created the requirement for e-discovery—the requirement to archive and retrieve electronic records such as e-mail and instant messages.

This created an immediate need not just to archive information, but to automate its retrieval. This is because records must be produced in a timely way—and manual retrieval would take too long and be prohibitively expensive. The business risks of noncompliance are considerable: unlike many countries, US practice allows for potentially massive information disclosure obligations in litigation. Companies that fail to meet e-discovery requirements may experience repercussions that include legal sanctions. The implications are correspondingly onerous. Lawsuits may draw on information that is several years old, so businesses must have the capability to quickly search and access archived information as well as current data. E-discovery is further complicated by the growth of cloud computing models such as software as a service (SaaS). As organizations outsource more business processes and data to cloud service suppliers, they need to ensure that their suppliers comply with their e-discovery needs.

Expanding Scope of Regulation

The regulatory universe continues to expand, with the likelihood of more regulations that explicitly address IT, as new technologies emerge and governments try to control its use and inevitable misuse.

Some technology-specific regulations have been triggered by specific events. In India, for example, after terrorists used unsecured Wi-Fi access points to communicate information about their attacks, the government created a legal requirement that any access point must be secured (Government of India Department of Telecommunications 2009).

In other countries, businesses that operate unsecured Wi-Fi access points—a common way to provide Internet access for visitors—may find themselves facing other legal problems. For example, unscrupulous individuals may tap into the network to access web sites for purposes such as illegally downloading music or pornography. Access appears to originate from the company hosting the access point, which may then find itself on the receiving end of correspondence or raids from the music industry or government agencies.

The Rapid Proliferation of Information and Devices

The computing environment is growing as rapidly as the regulatory environment. The sheer volume of information is exploding, and it is being stored across a rapidly growing array of portable computing devices.

This is a dramatic acceleration and expansion of a long-running trend that began when businesses first started equipping employees with desktop and then laptop PCs. Now, employees are using millions of smartphones and other devices, such as tablets, to access and store information.

At the same time, the boundaries between work and personal technology are dissolving. Whether businesses officially allow it or not, employees are increasingly using their personal devices for work—sending e-mails from and storing information on their personal smartphones and computers. Furthermore, people may forward e-mail from business accounts to personal accounts created on external systems—without considering that when they signed up for the personal account, they agreed to a license that allows the external provider to scrutinize their e-mails.

The use of personal technology can considerably enhance business productivity because employees can now communicate from anywhere at any time. However, this also creates a more complex, fragmented environment with more potential points of attack. Information is now exposed on millions of new devices and disparate external networks, many of which do not have the same type of security controls as corporate PCs—and all of which are outside corporate network firewalls.

Statistics show that malware producers are already responding to the growing popularity of these new devices; security firm McAfee (owned by Intel) (2011) reported significant growth in malware targeting mobile devices during the second quarter of 2011—with a 76 percent increase in malware aimed at devices running Google's Android software.

We can expect an ever-growing variety of networked devices. In fact, in the not too distant future, almost any device with a power supply might have a network address and be capable of communicating—and being attacked—over the Internet.

Already, cars contain dozens of control computers that communicate over internal networks. Some have IP addresses, and with a mobile phone app, owners can remotely control a variety of functions, including starting the car. Researchers have shown that it's possible to insert malicious code into a car's computers to control the brakes and accelerator. They have also shown that navigation systems in cars can be spoofed to send the driver to the wrong destination. Consider the possibilities if a family member is driving the car, or a company executive.

The boundaries between work and personal lives are dissolving in other ways, too. Employees store more information on the Internet—on business and consumer social media sites, for example—than ever before. These sites have become powerful tools for communicating with audiences outside the corporate firewall.

However, just as there's an industry gathering and analyzing personal information for marketing purposes, information on the Web can be used for competitive intelligence or for less legitimate purposes. Users store snippets of information in multiple places on the Web. Though each of these snippets may not provide much information, when pieced together, they can provide new intelligence—not just about the individual, but also about the organization to which the person belongs. Each item is like a single pixel in a digital picture. Alone, it doesn't convey much information; but step back—aggregating information from a wider range of sources—and multiple pixels combine to form a portrait. In the same way, pieces of information strewn across a variety of unrelated web sites—the name of a department, workmates, pet names that might be used as passwords—can be linked together to create a picture of an individual and used for malicious purposes.

The Changing Threat Landscape

The threat landscape is evolving rapidly, with an increase in highly organized and well-funded groups capable of executing sustained attacks to achieve long-term goals. Such a group is thought to have created Stuxnet, a sophisticated worm that targeted specific industrial systems and is suspected to have set back the Iranian nuclear program by as much as two years. These attackers, generally known as *advanced persistent threats* (APTs), were originally focused mainly on governments. However, more recent data indicates that APTs are now targeting private-sector organizations, with the goal of grabbing proprietary data and intellectual property.

A related trend is the steady rise of organized cybercrime online. This is entirely logical. As the exchange of money and information has moved online, organized crime has followed, focusing on theft of valuable assets such as intellectual property. This has spawned a mature malware industry that increasingly resembles the legitimate software industry, complete with a broad set of services, guarantees, and price competition among suppliers.

Stealthy Malware

This evolving set of threat agents is using new, more sophisticated tools and methods to mount attacks. Once upon a time, attackers were amateurish—often driven by personal motives such as the prestige of bringing down a big company's network. Accordingly, the arrival of malware on a user's machine was easy to detect: the malware announced itself with icons or messages, and the system often became unusable.

Now the trend is toward malware that is stealthy and uses sophisticated techniques to avoid detection. Attackers plant malware that lies undetected over a long period while it captures information. Another common technique is to quietly spread malware by injecting malicious code into an unsuspecting company's web site; users who visit the site then unknowingly download the code onto their systems.

Accompanying this is a shift from spam mass e-mails to carefully crafted attacks aimed at individuals or specific groups: so-called *spearphishing*. These typically use social engineering techniques, such as providing enough contextual or personal information in an e-mail to tempt people to download malware or click on a link to an infected web site created specifically for that purpose.

Though more expensive to mount, spearphishing attacks are growing because they can be enormously profitable to cybercriminals. In a report entitled "Email Attacks: This Time It's Personal," Cisco Security Intelligence Operations (2011) noted that gains from traditional mass e-mail attacks shrank by 50 percent to USD 500 million due to a number of factors, including the enforced shutdown of several major spam operations. Meanwhile, spearphishing attacks, which can net ten times the profit of a mass attack, tripled, and personalized malicious attacks increased fourfold, costing organizations worldwide about USD 1.29 billion annually—more than double the overall financial impact of mass e-mail attacks. We can expect these stealthy and targeted attacks to continue, with new methods emerging as necessary to circumvent defenses.

Compromise Is Inevitable

The result of this intersection of trends—increasingly sophisticated attackers and methods combined with the enormous proliferation of devices and information—is that traditional prevention methods such as firewalls are no longer adequate. In fact, enterprises need to assume that compromise is inevitable; no defenses can be entirely effective.

I've summarized the reasons why in the following Six Irrefutable Laws of Information Security (with acknowledgements to Culp [2000], Venables [2008], Lindstrom [2008], and other sources):

- Law #1: *Information wants to be free.* People want to talk, post, and share information—and they increase risk by doing so. Some examples:

  A senior executive at a major technology company updated his profile on a business social networking site. In doing so, he inadvertently pre-announced a shift in his employer's strategy—a mistake that was promptly and gleefully picked up by the press.

  An employee found a novel way to fix a piece of equipment more quickly, and—to help others across the company—decided to videotape the procedure. Because video files are so large, it didn't make sense to e-mail the video, so the employee posted it online. Unfortunately, by doing so, he exposed confidential information.

  At one time or another, many people have experienced this disconcerting event: when composing a message, the e-mail software helpfully autofills the address field, but it selects the wrong name from the address book. You hit send without realizing the error, thus dispatching a company-confidential message to someone outside the organization.

  It's worth noting that that this rule is not new. Information has always wanted to be free: think of the World War II slogan "loose lips sink ships." People communicate, and sometimes they share more information than they should. It's just the methods that have changed—and the fact that, with the Internet, a carelessly mentioned detail is instantly available to anyone across the globe.

- Law #2: *Code wants to be wrong.* We will never have 100-percent error-free software. In fact, the more widely used the software, the more malicious individuals will hunt for vulnerabilities in the code. They have found and exploited errors in the world's most widely used web sites, productivity applications, and enterprise business software.

- Law #3: *Services want to be on.* On any computer, some background processes always need to be running, and these can be exploited by attackers. These could even be security software processes used for everyday activities like keeping systems up-to-date with software patches or monitoring for malware.

- Law #4: *Users want to click.* People naturally tend to click when they see links, buttons, or prompts. Malware creators know this, and they take advantage of it. In fact, the entire phishing industry is based on the assumption that users will click on enticing e-mails, web sites, or pop-up ads, triggering the download of malicious code to their systems. The evolution of highly targeted attacks such as spearphishing has taken this to a new level, as when e-mails purporting to be letters discussing legal action from a circuit court were sent to senior executives at a number of companies.

- Law #5: *Fake antivirus software—designed to actually spread viruses and malware—is becoming a growing menace online.* Posting such fake software on the Web is proving to be an effective way for bad guys to get users to install malware on work and home PCs. According to Google researchers, fake antivirus software accounted for 15 percent of malicious content detected on web sites in a recent 13-month period (Rajab 2010).

  Even a security feature can be used for harm. Security tools can be exploited by attackers, just like other software. This means that laws 2, 3, and 4 are true for security capabilities, too.

  According to the *San Francisco Chronicle* (Van Derbeken 2008), the network engineer who built San Francisco's new multimillion-dollar computer network locked the city out of its own network—refusing to divulge the passwords—when he heard about impending layoffs.

  More recently, the systems of a well-known provider of security certificates were compromised. Beyond announcing that the compromise had occurred, the provider didn't share much information about the event, leaving the businesses who had purchased the certificates in an odd position of not knowing whether their systems were secure or not. This is like hearing that your local locksmith has been burgled—without details about exactly was taken—and trying to decide whether you should immediately invest in new locks or wait to see whether you experience an attempted burglary yourself.

- Law #6: *The efficacy of a control deteriorates with time.* Once put in place, security controls tend to remain static—while the environment in which they operate is dynamic. As a result, a control's ability to produce the intended effect diminishes over time, and the effectiveness of the controls progressively degrades.

  This happens for a variety of reasons. Some are internal: there's a tendency to "set and forget"—to install applications and then fail to update them with security patches or to properly maintain access lists.

There are also external reasons for this trend. Recently, researchers at the University of Pennsylvania analyzed the rate at which vulnerabilities were discovered following 700 major software releases (Clark et al. 2010). They found that, in most cases, there was a honeymoon period, averaging about 110 days, during which time relatively few vulnerabilities appeared. After this period, the discovery rate increased exponentially. Their conclusion: the honeymoon essentially represented the hackers' learning curve!

A New Approach to Managing Risk

Given the ever-broadening role of technology and the resulting information-related business risk, we need a new approach to information security built on the concept of protecting to enable. Because compromise is inevitable, managing risk and surviving compromise are key elements of this strategy. This approach should:

- *Incorporate privacy and regulatory compliance by design, to encompass the full scope of business risk.* Also, because technology is now key to every business process, the information security organization must work closely with other business groups to understand and manage risk.

- *Recognize that people and information—not the enterprise network boundary—are the security perimeter.* Information is no longer restricted to tightly managed systems within data centers; it now also resides outside the firewall, on users' personal devices, and on the Internet. Managing risk therefore requires a range of new tools, including user awareness and effective security controls for personal devices.

- Be dynamic and flexible enough to quickly adapt to new technologies and threats. To provide maximum benefit to users, we need to be able to quickly accommodate new devices as they emerge. Our security approach must also be flexible to respond to the changing threat landscape: a static model will inevitably be overtaken by the dynamic nature of threats.

Above all, we need to accomplish a shift in thinking, adjusting our primary focus to enabling the business, and then thinking creatively about how we can do so while managing the risk. Information is the central nervous system of the company. Our role is to provide the protection that enables information to flow freely.

CHAPTER 2

The Misperception of Risk

The moment we want to believe something, we suddenly see all the arguments for it, and become blind to the arguments against it.

—George Bernard Shaw

One hundred years ago, the "unsinkable" *Titanic* foundered after striking an iceberg off the coast of Newfoundland. More than 1,500 people died in what became one of the deadliest maritime accidents ever. Several factors contributed to this massive death toll, but perhaps the most critical was that there simply weren't enough lifeboats. The ship carried 2,224 people, but fewer than half of them could squeeze into the boats.

As we know, passengers who didn't get a spot in one of those lifeboats quickly died in the freezing waters of the North Atlantic. What's less well known is that the *Titanic's* supply of lifeboats was in full compliance with the British marine regulations in force at time. The law required the ship to carry 16 lifeboats; the *Titanic* actually had 20 lifeboats.

The ship's owners did a good job of providing enough boats to address the regulatory risk of noncompliance. Unfortunately, meeting regulatory requirements did little to prevent the tragic loss of life.

This is a case of *misperception of risk*. The owners focused on mitigating the regulatory risk, apparently blind to the much larger risk of disaster. A sad footnote: reports suggest the *Titanic* had enough capacity to easily add enough lifeboats for everyone on board, had the owners chosen to do so.

What does this example have to do with information security? We encounter misperceptions every day within the realm of enterprise risk and security. Furthermore, unless we mitigate these misperceptions, they can have disastrous consequences. As a result, I believe the misperception of risk is the most significant vulnerability facing enterprises today.

The Subjectivity of Risk Perception

As security professionals, we tend to think about objective ways to estimate risk—to assess the likelihood and extent of harm that can occur due to specific threats and vulnerabilities.

But in reality, the way people perceive risk has a strong subjective component. Economic and psychological factors greatly affect how each of us perceives the likelihood and potential impact of harm from specific actions or situations. Within an organization, each individual's perception of risk varies depending on his or her job role, goals, background, and peer group. This means managers, security professionals, and end users all may have a different view of the risk associated with a specific technology or action.

Misperceiving risk has serious consequences because our actions are shaped by our perception of risk. An employee may think posting personal and work-related information on a social-media site is relatively harmless. However, hackers might use this publicly available information in phishing e-mails to gain access to enterprise systems via the employee's computer, ultimately resulting in detrimental security breaches.

End users are not the only members of the organization who can misperceive risk. Everyone is capable of misperceiving risk, including risk and security professionals. As I'll explain later in this chapter, misperceptions occur at the group level as well as the individual level. Members of a group may share the same bias in their perception of risk and benefit.

The decisions that result from these misperceptions can weaken the entire organization's security posture. If an organization underestimates a risk, it will under spend on controls to mitigate that risk, increasing the likelihood and potential impact of major problems such as data breaches. On the other hand, if the organization overestimates a risk, it will allocate a disproportionately large share of its security resources to the risk, leaving other parts of the risk landscape underprotected.

In this chapter, I'll discuss how and why different people within an organization misperceive risk—whether they are acting as information technology users, security professionals, or managerial decision makers. To explore these misperceptions, I've drawn on research across the broader field of risk psychology, notably *The Psychology of Risk*, a book by Professor Dame Glynis Breakwell, Vice Chancellor of the University of Bath (Cambridge University Press, 2007). I'll examine how these ideas about risk perception apply to information risk and security. I'll explain some of the consequences of those misperceptions, and I'll discuss some of the ways an organization can address them.

How Employees Misperceive Risk

Research shows that if we like an activity, we tend to judge its benefits to be high and its risk to be low (Slovic 2010). Conversely, if we dislike the activity, we judge it as low-benefit and high-risk. Because of this, the perception of risk by individuals and groups within an organization tends to be biased by their preferences, roles, and objectives. Everyone is trying to achieve their individual or group goals within the organization, so they tend to see activities and technologies that support those goals as beneficial, and therefore they tend to underestimate the risk.

So if employees like social media, their attraction to the technology skews their perception of benefit and risk. Because they judge the benefit to be high and the risk to be low, they feel comfortable posting information such as their job title, location, and even the projects they're working on. They may even allow sites to capture their location, using the global positioning system in their cell phone, and display the location in real time.

Unfortunately, these employees may not think about how a malicious individual could use the information. Today, as we've seen, an individual's use of technology can harm not only the individual, but the entire organization. Attackers exploit publicly available personal information to craft spearphishing e-mails that are particularly convincing because they appear to demonstrate a relationship with the recipient, making the employee more likely to click on a link that downloads malware to the system. From there, the attack spreads to the rest of the corporate network. In addition, information posted by individuals is now routinely aggregated, analyzed to identify patterns, and sold, often to a company's competitors.

The risk and security team may also misperceive the risk of social media, but in the opposite direction—they overestimate the risk and underestimate the benefits. They may not like social media because it creates vulnerabilities, and their perception then drives them to focus on minimizing the risk by trying to block the use of the technology.

Other psychological factors also come into play in shaping end users' risk perception. People in general tend to believe they are personally less likely than others to experience negative events, and more likely to experience positive events, leading to a sense of personal invulnerability (Breakwell 2007). In addition, users also are more likely to behave in risky ways if their colleagues do so. "It's conformity—being seen to be doing what everybody else is doing," Breakwell says (pers. comm.). Many social media sites encourage this conformist tendency—if all your friends are using a social media site, you're likely to join the site too because it enables you to see what they are doing and share information with them more easily.

The likelihood that individuals will behave in ways risky to the organization also increases when their individual interests don't align with the company's. This divergence is most likely when employees are discontented, resentful, demoralized, or simply don't trust IT or the broader organization.

In economic theory, the problem resulting from this lack of alignment is known as a *moral hazard*: a situation in which someone behaves differently from the way they would if they were fully exposed to the risk. A useful moral hazard analogy is renting a car with full insurance coverage. People are likely to be less careful with the rental car than they would be with their own car if they're not responsible for the consequences. The attitude is "if it's not mine, it doesn't matter."

In the realm of enterprise IT, moral hazards may be a bigger concern than many appreciate. A Cisco survey (2011a) found that 61 percent of employees felt they were not responsible for protecting information and devices, believing instead that their IT groups or IT service providers were accountable. Ominously, 70 percent of these surveyed employees said they frequently ignored IT policies.

One indicator of the extent of moral hazard within an organization may be how employees treat company-provided laptops. Higher-than-average loss or damage rates might suggest employees don't care about the laptops and may be an indication they don't care about other corporate assets either. As I'll discuss in Chapter 5, I believe allowing reasonable personal use of laptops can help reduce the risk of moral hazard because it aligns personal interests with those of the organization.

More broadly, organizations can address the moral hazard issue by taking steps to align the goals and concerns of everyone involved: end users, information security professionals, and executives. This returns to the theme of the book—as information security professionals, our mission is to Protect to Enable. This mission aligns our security goals with those of the business. It helps maintain the perception of shared values. Research suggests that people with whom we share values are deemed more trustworthy (Breakwell 2007, 143). If employees trust us, they are more likely to believe our warnings and act on our recommendations.

One further point to remember is that everyone in the organization, regardless of the job role, is an end user. Therefore, we can all fall prey to the same tendencies. For example, we may be attracted to new consumer technologies and tend to ignore the risks.

How Security Professionals Misperceive Risk

While end users tend to underestimate the risks of a desirable activity or technology, security professionals sometimes display the opposite tendency. We focus obsessively on the information risk associated with a specific threat or vulnerability. In doing so, we completely miss bigger risks.

This phenomenon is known as *target fixation*—a term originally coined to describe a situation in which fighter-bomber pilots focus so intently on a target during a strafing or bombing run that they fail to notice the bigger risk to themselves and crash into the target as a result (Colgan 2010, 44). As information security professionals, we can develop a similar fixation. We focus so intently on one risk that our awareness of larger hazards is diminished. This target fixation can also occur in other groups with "control" functions within the organization, such as internal audit, legal compliance, and corporate risk management.

Here is an example from our own experience at Intel, which I'll discuss further in Chapter 9. Several years ago, we discovered that malware had been introduced onto our network from an employee's personal computer. We became so focused on this source of danger that we eliminated all personal devices from our network. We further fueled our target fixation by labeling these devices non-Intel managed systems (NIMS), a term that reflected the frustration over our lack of control. I vowed we would never again allow network access from devices that we didn't fully control.

However, by becoming fixated on a single threat, we may have created some larger risks and additional costs. For example, we needed to issue contract employees with corporate PCs, each of which allowed broader access to the Intel environment. If we had instead focused on how we could provide limited access to the environment from "untrusted" devices, we might have managed the risk with lower total cost and obtained a head start in developing a key aspect of our current security strategy, as I'll describe in Chapter 8.

As security professionals, we also may misperceive risk due to the tendency to "set and forget" security controls. This common security loophole is described in the sixth Irrefutable Law of Information Security in Chapter 1, which states that the efficacy of a control deteriorates with time. Once in place, controls tend to remain static, while the threats they are intended to mitigate continue to evolve and change, sometimes in very dynamic ways. Controls that are initially very effective can become inadequate over time. Ultimately, an adverse event may occur and may even have disastrous consequences.

Think about the history of major oil tanker spills. For years, regulations allowed tankers to be built with a single hull, instead of a double (inner and outer) hull to provide additional protection in the event of a leak. Meanwhile, tankers grew steadily larger because bigger ships could transport oil more efficiently than smaller ones. It wasn't until the *Exxon Valdez* ran aground, puncturing its hull and creating a giant oil leak that contaminated huge stretches of Alaska's coast, that authorities were spurred to create new regulations requiring double hulls in oil tankers (EPA 2011).

Within enterprise IT, a typical "set and forget" error is the failure to keep controls up-to-date, particularly if the controls are designed to mitigate a relatively low risk. A case in point: *distributed denial of service (DDoS)* threats were a big concern more than a decade ago, due to widely publicized attacks by worms such as Code Red, Nimda, and SQL Slammer. These attacks disabled corporate web sites or flooded internal networks by overloading them with requests. To mitigate the availability risk, many organizations invested in defenses against DDoS attacks.

Over time, however, DDoS attacks became less frequent, and organizations were assailed by newer threats. With limited resources, information security groups focused on mitigating these new threats rather than continuing to build defenses against DDoS attacks. At the same time, though, businesses were increasing their online presence. Web sites evolved from being used primarily for advertising and displaying static corporate information to managing business-critical data and applications. Some organizations began conducting all their business online. Even traditional brick-and-mortar businesses moved customer support, order management, and other critical business processes onto the Web. The larger online presence multiplied the potential impact of a successful attack. As a result, when DDoS attacks from a variety of groups resurfaced in the past few years, they created even greater disruption to business operations as well as damage to corporate brands.

Another example: over the past few years, many organizations have become much more diligent about scrubbing data from the hard drives of old computers before disposing of them or reselling them. But they failed to follow similar precautions for other business devices that have evolved to include hard drives.

Nearly every digital copier contains a drive storing an image of each document copied, scanned, or e-mailed by the machine. When CBS News reporters visited a company that specialized in reselling used copiers, they found businesses and agencies had discarded machines containing lists of wanted sex offenders, drug raid targets, pay stubs with Social Security numbers, and check images. One copier's hard drive even contained 300 pages of individual medical records, including a cancer diagnosis, which is a potential breach of federal privacy law (Keteyian 2010).

MISMATCHING CONTROLS TO THREATS

Businesses sometimes devote considerable time and resources to implement security controls that are completely irrelevant to the threats the companies are trying to mitigate. These mismatches reveal a lack of understanding of the security technology and the threat. The controls may further add to the risk by providing a false sense of security. In reality, deploying the wrong control is like carrying a lightning rod to protect oneself from getting wet in a storm.

Typical mismatches include:

- Using firewalls to prevent data theft from applications that are allowed to operate through the firewall

- Using standard antivirus tools that are effective only against previously identified threats, to protect against zero-day attacks

- Using controls at the operating-system level to detect application-layer attacks

This mismatch does not mean that these controls are worthless. It simply means that if our goal is to deal with a specific threat, we must understand both the attacks and the controls well enough to identify which controls are applicable, and where it is necessary to add other controls. For example, if a firewall cannot prevent attacks against an application, we might deploy an additional control behind the firewall.

How Decision Makers Misperceive Risk

A manager makes decisions based on information from technical specialists and other experts. Therefore, the decisions managers make are only as good as the information they receive. Decision makers can misperceive risk when their decisions are based on biased or incomplete information.

Bias can influence these decisions every day. If people are trying to sell a particular proposal or point of view to their manager, what are they likely to do? They tend to select data supporting their arguments and often ignore data contradicting those arguments.

The danger of misperception is particularly acute when decision makers rely on a narrow range of sources who all share similar viewpoints. Without obtaining a diversity of viewpoints, managers don't get a full picture of the risk. Like-minded individuals tend to agree with each other, as you might expect. When a group is composed solely of people with similar backgrounds and viewpoints, it may be particularly prone to group polarization (Breakwell 2007, 99) and the group's decision may be more extreme than the mean of their individual views. This problem may be especially acute when the people involved share the same mental model of the world, as is likely to be the case when the group consists only of specialists from the same organization.

An even broader concern is how a focus on business goals can drive people to make unethical decisions. When these decisions are made by managers at the organizational level rather than at the individual level, the impact is compounded by the potential for widespread disaster.

After the *Challenger* space shuttle exploded in 1986, extensive post-crash analysis revealed the tragedy was caused because an O-ring on one of the shuttle's booster rockets failed to seal due to the low ambient temperature at launch time.

However, it subsequently emerged that engineers had warned of the potential danger before the launch. Engineers from NASA contractor Morton Thiokol recommended the shuttle not be launched at low temperatures after analyzing data that indicated a link between low temperatures and O-ring problems. After NASA responded negatively to the engineers' recommendation, Morton Thiokol's general manager reportedly decided to treat the question of whether to launch was a "management decision." Against the objections of their own engineers, Morton Thiokol's managers then recommended NASA go ahead and launch, and NASA quickly accepted this recommendation (Bazerman and Tenbrunsel 2011, 13–16).

For Morton Thiokol's managers, the desire to meet the business goal of pleasing the company's customer, NASA, apparently caused the ethical dimensions of the problem to fade from consideration—with terrible consequences.

According to Tenbrunsel, this "ethical fading" is not uncommon. The way a decision is framed can limit our perspective. If the decision is framed purely in terms of meeting business goals, ethical considerations may fade from view. In fact, we may become blind to the fact that we are confronting an ethical problem at all (Joffe-Walt and Spiegel 2012).

Another infamous ethical lapse involved the Ford Pinto, whose gas tank exploded in a number of rear-end collisions, resulting in fatalities. As Bazerman and Tenbrunsel describe (2011, 69–71), Ford discovered the dangers in preproduction testing. However, facing intense business competition, the company decided to go ahead with manufacturing anyway. The decision was based on a cost-benefit analysis. Ford apparently considered the choice as a business decision rather than an ethical decision and determined it would be cheaper to pay off lawsuits than make the repair. The impact of dehumanizing this risk decision was disastrous.

In the past, many information technology risk decisions have often been considered only in terms of their potential business impact. As information technology is integrated into more and more products, decisions about information risk will increasingly affect the lives of millions of people, making it essential to consider the ethical as well as the business dimensions of information risks. It becomes even more important that we, as CISOs, keep ethical considerations to the forefront. What is the potential impact of a security breach when a car's sensors and control systems can be accessed via the Internet? Or when medical life-support equipment can be remotely controlled using wireless links?

How to Mitigate the Misperception of Risk

It should be apparent by now that the tendency to misperceive risk is universal. We need to find ways to help compensate for this misperception, given that it is our job to manage risk. As security professionals and managers, how can we mitigate the misperception of risk?

We can start by ensuring we include a diversity of viewpoints when making risk management decisions. Whenever possible, we should involve a broad cross-section of individuals representing groups across the organization. This diversity helps compensate for individual biases.

However, assembling the right mix of people is only the first step in building a more complete picture of risk. As information security professionals, we need to ensure that the discussion brings up new perspectives and views. We must ask penetrating questions designed to bring alternative viewpoints to the surface. We need to continually seek out the minority report, the view that is contrary to perceived wisdom. If the majority is telling me to turn right, are we missing something important that we'd find out by turning left?

This questioning counteracts the inevitable bias due to target fixation. We can also help counter target fixation by simply recognizing it exists, and then consciously trying to see the problem from someone else's viewpoint.

Uncovering New Perspectives During Risk Assessments

Risk assessment models can be valuable tools for helping to evaluate risks and to prioritize security resources. But all models have limitations. If we base our decisions solely on the results generated by a model, we may miss important risks.

At Intel, we typically use a risk assessment model based on a standard methodology. The model scores each risk using the formula:

```
Impact of Asset Loss × Probability of Threat × Vulnerability Exposure =
Total Risk Points
```

For each risk, we assign a rating to each of the three contributing factors in the formula. To illustrate, I'll use a scale of 1 to 5. A high-value asset, such as a microprocessor design, might warrant a rating of 5.

We then multiply the three ratings to obtain the total risk points. In this example, the maximum possible risk score is therefore 53, or 125.

A simple approach to risk management, using the output of the model, would be to divide the security budget among the highest-scoring risks.

The model is valuable because it provides a consistent method for helping compare and prioritize a broad spectrum of risks. However, allocating resources based only on the overall risk score can miss potentially disastrous "black swan" events that have very low probability but extremely high impact (Taleb 2007). Because the formula simply multiplies three ratings to obtain the overall score, black swans tend not to score as highly as lower-impact events with higher probability.

To counteract this problem, we can examine the information in the model in more detail, from different perspectives. We can create a list of the 20 most valuable assets and consider whether they need additional controls. In the same way, we can examine the top threats and vulnerability areas.

The point is that any model used to calculate risk should be used as a framework to drive a dialogue about all the variables and options, rather than as a tool that generates the answers to our problems. By discussing the issues from a variety of perspectives, we may identify important concerns we'd miss if we simply look at the overall risk scores.

Before I moved into the information security field, I worked in finance. In our finance group, we found the same principle held true when conducting ROI (return on investment) analysis. Our ROI model generated forecasts. However, it was by discussing the model's assumptions that we determined whether or not the model's predicted financial returns were reasonable.

Another method for prioritizing information systems risk management is to examine systems from the perspective of critical business processes and to consider the impact of a loss of confidentiality, integrity, or availability.

An application that prints shipping labels may initially appear to be low priority because it is small, inexpensive, and doesn't contain confidential data—it simply takes the information it needs from a customer information system on the network. However, if it's unavailable because the network is experiencing problems, the impact is huge because the company cannot ship products.

The potential impact to a business process of losing confidentiality, integrity, or availability may also vary depending on the stage of the business cycle. Consider a payroll system. Information confidentiality and integrity are always important; but availability is exceptionally critical on payday.

Communication Is Essential

Communication is an essential part of any strategy to mitigate the misperception of risk. To alter the way people behave, we need to change their perception of risk. To effect that change, we must communicate with them.

Changing perceptions is difficult. We may need to address long-held preconceptions about what is risky and what is not. Once people form an initial estimate of risk, they can be remarkably resistant to adjusting their perception, even when given new information (Breakwell 2007, 59).

In addition, each person may have a different perception of risk. To communicate effectively, we may need to understand an individual's viewpoint and then tailor our communication accordingly. Consider the example of taking laptops to countries with a high risk of information theft (see sidebar). People who are extremely concerned may need a patient, thorough explanation of the risks and benefits of taking their laptop versus leaving it in the office. A less fearful individual may just need a quick reassurance and a few basic facts.

Though changing risk perceptions can be challenging, we don't have any choice but to try. Employees will use social media whether we like it or not. When they do, they may not only put themselves at risk; they could be putting the company at risk too, if they are not careful.

Communication can reduce the issue of misperception due to asymmetry of information. This asymmetry is created when security professionals know about risks but don't share the information with end users within their organization. When two parties differ in their knowledge of a threat or vulnerability, their perception of risk is likely to differ also. In other words, it is difficult for users to care about a hazard if they don't even know it exists.

To succeed in changing users' perceptions, we must communicate in ways that engage them, using language they understand rather than technical jargon. At Intel, we have employed entertaining, interactive video tools to help engage users and teach them how to spot dangers such as phishing web sites. As I'll explain further in Chapter 5, we've found these methods have been highly effective in changing users' awareness and perceptions, and ultimately in shaping their behavior.

Patiently explaining to users the consequences of their actions can also help shape their perception of risk. In some countries, pirating software is so commonplace that it is almost an accepted part of the culture. This poses a problem for many multinational companies. Employees in these countries may not even believe copying software is wrong, let alone view it as an illegal act. It can be useful to describe the potential consequences of copyright infringement for the individual and for the organization. We can explain to employees that a decision to pirate software can expose the company to software license compliance risks. The consequences may be even more far-reaching if the copied software is then incorporated into the company's technology-based products or services. If a product is discovered to include stolen software, the company may be unable to ship it to customers, which means a significant loss of revenue. Of course, employees may experience personal consequences too: if they copy software, they run a high risk of losing their jobs.

Organizations as a whole may also be blind to risks, or simply choose to ignore them. One way to overcome this misperception is to patiently build up a list of examples showing how other organizations ignored similar risks and experienced adverse consequences as a result, according to Breakwell, the University of Bath psychologist (pers. comm. 2012). The more examples in the list, the harder they are to ignore.

"Organizations stick their heads in the sand, ostrich-like," she says. "But if you have a database of examples illustrating where things have gone wrong elsewhere, it becomes harder and harder to find enough sand to stick your head in."

CHALLENGING PRECONCEPTIONS: TAKING LAPTOPS TO HIGH-RISK COUNTRIES

It may be necessary to challenge perceived wisdom in order to expose a clear picture of the real risks, and consequently make the right decision.

Some companies react to the higher rates of intellectual property theft in certain countries by barring employees from taking their corporate laptops on business trips to those countries. In some cases, the companies issue employees with a new "clean" system from which all corporate data has been purged.

The goal is to prevent situations in which information theft might occur, such as when an employee leaves a laptop containing corporate data unattended in a hotel room. A malicious individual could then get physical access to the system and copy the data or implant software that will surreptitiously steal information over time.

But does preventing employees from taking their familiar laptops really solve the problem? Let's suppose we issue employees with a new, data-free laptop. To do their jobs, they'll still need to use this system to log into their corporate e-mail and other applications—providing an opportunity for hackers to intercept the network traffic.

Furthermore, if attackers really want to target an individual, they have ways to do it without gaining physical access to the system. With a spearphishing attack, they can induce the individual to click on a malicious link that remotely downloads malware.

Preventing employees from taking their laptops and information also deprives the organization of the key business benefits of using a full-featured portable computing device; employees will likely be less productive as a result. So when assessing the risks of traveling with mobile devices, an organization needs to think through the tradeoff between risk and benefit, including the cost of providing what they believe to be a "clean" system and the impact on the user.

Building Credibility

Ultimately, our ability to influence people's risk perception depends on our credibility. We need to build trusted relationships with executives and specialists across the organization to ensure our security concerns are seriously considered rather than seen as fearmongering or target fixation.

Trust is hard to create and easy to destroy. If business groups think we are providing unreliable and exaggerated information, will they trust us to provide their security? If we create a security scare about a threat that turns out to be irrelevant or overblown, we may be seen as just another source of misperception.

As I'll describe in more detail in Chapter 9, we can establish credibility by demonstrating consistency, striving for objectivity, and showing that we can accurately predict the real security issues affecting the organization, and then communicate them in an effective and timely way. Credibility is also built on the competence that comes from understanding the business and technology as well as possessing core security skills. As the scope and importance of information security continue to expand, creating this credibility provides an opportunity to step into a more valuable, high-profile role within the organization.

CHAPTER 3

■ ■ ■

Governance and Internal Partnerships

How to Sense, Interpret, and Act on Risk

If we are together nothing is impossible. If we are divided all will fail.

—Winston Churchill

To reduce cost, the company's human resources group wants to outsource payroll processing. At first glance, this might seem a low-risk decision. There's a clear business case, and outsourcing payroll doesn't create risks to corporate information assets such as intellectual property. Most businesses regard payroll as a commodity application, so they might tend to select the supplier who can process the payroll at the lowest cost.

But there's more to consider. Employees' personal information will be transferred to the outsourcer, creating new privacy concerns. And imagine the impact if thousands of our employees don't get paid because the supplier experiences system problems on payday and lacks adequate disaster recovery capabilities.

Clearly, the HR group owns the business process. However, outsourcing payroll can introduce risks for the entire business, not just for HR. Payroll processes involve systems that can create information risk. Outsourcing also involves procurement. The business needs a clear overview of all the factors, including the risks, in order to make the best decision. To provide this view, the HR, procurement, and information risk and security groups need to work together.

A typical organization makes many decisions that require this kind of internal partnership to manage the risk. A product group wants to outsource development work to bring a product to market more quickly. A marketing team wants to engage a developer for a new social media initiative.

Similar considerations also apply to internal technology transitions such as OS and application upgrades. Each new technology introduces new capabilities and risks. Often, the technology also includes features or options designed to reduce risk. By carefully analyzing the risk and security implications, including privacy and e-discovery considerations, we can help manage the risk of the transition, and we can often capitalize on the new features to improve the risk picture overall.

For example, when Intel IT was considering whether to migrate to Microsoft Windows 7, the information security team partnered with other groups in a broad evaluation of the OS. We identified several features that could improve security compared with previous versions of Microsoft Windows, and these security capabilities were an important factor in the decision to deploy Microsoft Windows 7 across Intel's enterprise environment (Fong, Kohlenberg, and Philips 2010).

The ability to make these decisions with an accurate view of risk depends on having the right organizational structure in place. In this chapter, I'll discuss two key aspects of this structure:

- *Clearly defined information risk governance.* Governance defines who makes decisions, who can block them, and who is allowed to provide input.

- *Strong partnerships.* Partnerships between the information risk and security team and other internal groups are critical in forming an accurate view of risk and managing risk overall. Some partnerships are formally defined as part of the risk governance structure; others are informal relationships. These formal and informal partnerships are so important that I'll dedicate a large part of the chapter to them.

Information Risk Governance

The Massachusetts Institute of Technology Center for Information Systems Research (MIT CISR) provides a useful definition of IT governance that neatly encapsulates some of the benefits: ". . . A framework for decision rights and accountability to encourage desirable behavior in the use of IT. Governance identifies who will make key IT decisions and how will they be held accountable."

Information risk governance is the component of IT governance that enables the organization to effectively sense, interpret, and act on risk. Information risk governance focuses on enabling the business while protecting the confidentiality, integrity, and availability of information—whether it is corporate data or personal information about employees or customers. Through partnerships between the information risk and security team and other groups, the organization can make tactical and strategic risk management decisions based on business priorities and a full view of the risks. We gather risk perspectives from across the organization and obtain buy-in to risk management decisions: a diversity of input leading to unity in decision-making.

To some people, the word governance may imply unnecessary bureaucracy, or perhaps even a dictatorial approach. It's true that any governance structure requires work to set up and maintain, but the value easily outweighs the administrative cost. When implemented well, a concise decision-making process can be a powerful mechanism for helping to achieve business objectives. Effective governance helps drive alignment and solid decision-making; it enables the organization to move more quickly while managing risk. As MIT CISR notes, "good governance is enabling and reduces bureaucracy and dysfunctional politics by formalizing organizational learning and thus avoiding the trap of making the same mistakes over and over again."

Research at MIT CISR shows that the more businesses leverage the structure, tools, and techniques of governance, the greater the potential benefits. In fact, MIT CISR's work suggests that firms with effective IT governance enjoy profits that average at least 20 percent higher than their competitors (MIT CISR 2012).

However, leveraging governance doesn't imply slavishly following rules and procedures. A few years ago, I encountered an IT professional who was regarded by some people, including himself, as one of the best managers in IT. He rigorously based his project decisions on the prescribed practices and procedures, and gathered the correct metrics for reporting progress. Yet the projects he was responsible for generally turned out to be large, expensive failures. His obsession with correct procedures often impeded, rather than facilitated, the projects he was working on.

To use an analogy, if you gave the same recipe to a top chef and an average cook, would you expect them to produce exactly the same result? Probably not. Expert chefs don't simply follow the rules; they continually make adjustments using their senses and experience to achieve the best results. The temperature of a cooking surface is not exactly uniform, so a chef may move the pots until they're simmering just right. Fresh ingredients vary from day to day; the experienced chef is alert to the differences and tweaks the recipe and seasoning accordingly.

Like recipes, IT policies provide a valuable framework. However, their value lies in what we can achieve by following the guidelines. Sometimes we need to make adjustments based on sensing changes in business needs. Otherwise, like the procedure-obsessed IT project manager, we may scrupulously adhere to the rules but fail to achieve the desired outcome.

This is one reason that partnerships are so critical. They provide channels for dialogue, helping us sense changing business priorities so that we mitigate risk based on those priorities rather than our preconceptions.

Without a governance structure that facilitates this dialogue, organizations may take too rigid an approach when applying controls to manage and mitigate risks. For example, some security groups try to ban the business use of social media due to the risks, but attempting to stop the use of external social media web sites is counterproductive and, in any case, impossible. At Intel, we have found it's more effective to embrace social media and shape the way that employees use it, as I'll describe in Chapter 5. This approach, developed in partnership with other internal groups, enables the organization to enjoy the benefits of social media while managing the risk.

Finding the Right Governance Structure

It's important to find an information risk governance structure that fits the organization and the overall way IT is governed. As discussed in the sidebar and summarized in Table 3-1, MIT CISR has conducted some interesting research to identify IT governance archetypes (Weill and Ross 2000). These archetypes may be useful when thinking about information risk management based on how your own organization governs IT.

Table 3-1. *IT Governance Archetypes*

Style	Who has decision or input rights
Business Monarchy	A group of business or individual executives (CxOs). Includes committees of senior business executives (may include CIO)
IT Monarchy	IT executives
Feudal	Business unit leaders, key process owners, or their delegates
Federal	C-level executives and business groups; may also include IT executives. Equivalent of central and state governments working together
IT Duopoly	IT executives and one other group (for example, CxO or business unit leaders)
Anarchy	Each individual user

Source: Weill and Ross 2000

IT GOVERNANCE ARCHETYPES

As defined in Weill and Ross 2000, 59

The way an organization governs information risk management must mesh with its overall IT governance. There's no single IT governance model, but in the influential book *IT Governance*, researchers at Massachusetts Institute of Technology Center for Information Systems Research described several archetypal models based on deliberately provocative political archetypes.

These archetypes may be useful when considering how to implement a risk governance structure that fits the organization's IT governance style.

In practice, organizations may have shifted between different IT governance models over time—from an IT monarchy during the mainframe era, toward a feudal model or business monarchy as distributed systems emerged, then swinging back to a federal model as they recognized there's a role for centralized IT. With the adoption of cloud computing, some organizations are now moving toward a business monarchy.

Further complicating the picture, organizations may simultaneously use multiple governance models for different aspects of IT: the enterprise network might be managed as an IT monarchy, while a business monarchy governs the systems that connect to the network.

If an organization's IT governance model already includes strong links between IT and business groups, the CISO may be able to leverage those existing linkages to build partnerships for managing information risk. This might be the case in organizations at which the governance model resembles the federal or duopoly archetypes described in the sidebar, with IT and business groups both directly involved in IT governance. If the organization more closely fits the IT monarchy archetype (IT is run as a centralized function with weaker links to business groups), the CISO may need to proactively establish new partnerships with business managers.

Intel's Information Risk Governance

At Intel, as at most large companies, risk is decentralized: at any one time, our company is planning or managing many technology-related initiatives and events across practically every part of the business. Therefore, we need decentralized risk management processes. But at the same time, we need a broad centralized view of the dynamic risk landscape.

Our goal is to implement a comprehensive and balanced approach to risk management. To achieve this goal, our approach includes a large number of risk management activities grouped into five broad focus areas, as shown in Figure 3-1: oversight, monitoring, engagements, operations, and strategic activities.

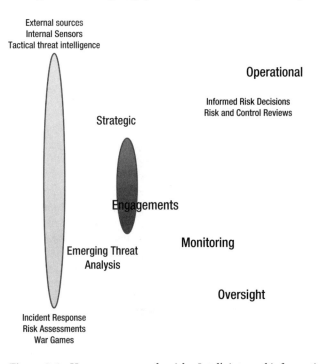

Figure 3-1. How we manage the risks: Intel's internal information risk management focus areas. Source: Intel Corporation, 2012

- *Oversight*. This area focuses on making informed risk decisions and reviewing risks. It includes committees and review boards that set strategic direction, and review key risk areas such as ethics, compliance, and corporate investigations.

- *Monitoring*. We monitor (sense) risk through external and internal sources. External sources include industry research and analysis. Internal sources include internal partners who inform us of new business risks or legal requirements. These internal sources also include our own security technology sensors.

- *Engagements*. We participate in industry workgroups and in partnerships and dialogues with trusted peer organizations. These external engagements provide a valuable risk-sensing function and help us influence key security initiatives. I'll discuss our external partnerships in more detail in Chapter 4.

- *Operations*. This area encompasses day-to-day risk management activities and processes, including risk assessments, incident response, and exercises such as war games.

- *Strategic*. Our strategic planning function interfaces with the other four components of governance. It includes our emerging threat analysis and long-range security architecture planning.

Our information risk governance structure is designed to support this balanced approach to risk management. It includes a large number of formal and informal partnerships and structures that help us sense, interpret, and act on risk. The partnerships also create a system of checks and balances by including diverse perspectives from different people across Intel, counteracting the inherent tendency for an individual group to introduce bias based on its own objectives (as I described in Chapter 2, we all have the potential to misperceive risk).

Building Internal Partnerships

By providing vehicles for dialogue and decision-making, internal partnerships enable information security teams to become more agile and responsive to business needs. The number of potential partnerships has grown as the scope of information risk has broadened to include a range of privacy and regulatory concerns as well as traditional security threats.

Today, Intel's information security team partners with many internal groups for a variety of functions, including risk management decisions, incident response, and monitoring. These groups include legal, finance, human resources, and business groups.

Partnerships may include formal structures such as standing committees and risk review boards, as described in the information risk governance section of this chapter. We also maintain a large number of informal and ad hoc relationships. These are created and maintained through everyday communication with people in other groups. We might initially contact a business group to understand the potential impact of an emerging area of legislation. The business group identifies risks and opportunities that we hadn't even considered. Our initial request thus sparks a dialogue about requirements and controls, and ultimately evolves into a partnership that helps us monitor risks and mitigate them.

Whether formal or informal, these partnerships should be treated and managed as valuable relationships. Partnerships with other internal groups are essential in helping to build trust, as I'll describe in Chapter 9. We also gain business acumen, which helps us play a more valuable role within the organization.

At Intel, partnerships have been critical to our success in understanding the broader risk picture, helping us sense, interpret, and act on risk. Through these relationships, other groups can act as additional eyes and ears for the information security group, helping us sense new risks, such as security threats and compliance concerns. For example, the HR legal group might alert us to an employment-related regulation that creates new compliance concerns. Information about risks flows in the other direction, too—we may alert our partner to new threats that we've encountered. As we leverage other groups to look out for our interests, they can also use us to look out for their interests. We also work with partners to interpret this shared information through analysis and decide how to act in response.

Establishing these relationships may create a far-reaching web of informal and formal partnerships across the organization. Although this web may appear complex, each partnership plays a role in helping us sense, interpret, or manage risk. Internal partnerships may focus on just one of the areas shown in Figure 3-1, or they may intersect multiple areas. For example, we partner with HR for incident response (operations), and to learn about new employment laws (monitoring). Multiple partnerships may also be required within each focus area: with the growing number of regulatory requirements, partnerships with internal groups such as HR legal, corporate security, and internal auditing become increasingly important and valuable in the area of operational investigations.

Because no two organizations are identical, each organization may require a different set of internal partnerships, depending on its structure and business needs. Every partnership should be created with a clear purpose. The organization should also clearly define who is involved and who makes the decisions. To determine the partnerships your information security group needs, as well as their structure and purpose, it may be useful to ask the following questions:

- Who do we need to partner with and why? To put it another way, who do I interact with every day, and why do I interact with them?

- What benefits do I receive from that interaction, and what benefits does my partner receive?

In the remainder of this chapter, I'll discuss some examples of important partnerships, describing how we can use them and the value they provide. I'll start by examining partnerships with "fellow travelers" who have complementary roles in managing business risk and liability: legal, finance, human resources, corporate security, and corporate risk management groups. Then, I'll examine partnerships with business group managers.

Legal

Legal groups are among the information security group's most important partners because of the many areas their roles intersect with ours. They own the responsibility for legal compliance and legal review. They interpret laws, analyzing the implications and relaying the relevant information to the rest of the organization. Key partnership areas include privacy, litigation, intellectual property, contracts, and compliance with financial regulations.

Privacy

As privacy regulations continue to grow in complexity and reach, many organizations need to comply with multiple requirements at local, regional, and national levels. Legal specialists across the organization can help us understand what's required in each geography, align policies and controls for protecting personal information, and decide how to manage responses in the event of a breach.

Even local regulations can have implications across the enterprise. For example, citizens of European countries are subject to European and national privacy laws and regulations. The simple transfer of European employee personnel information to a US-based server will trigger a need to comply with the EU data privacy laws regarding such transfer of employee information.

Litigation

As one might expect, it's essential to partner with legal specialists in situations where litigation is possible or already in process. Examples are investigations of security breaches, particularly when law enforcement is involved. Another area of partnership is in responding to subpoenas and litigation discovery orders; a legal group may need to work with the information security team in order to collect the required information. To ensure that data is available for discovery when needed, we may also need to collaborate with the legal group to implement appropriate data retention policies.

Intellectual Property and Data Classification

Many organizations use a data classification structure to protect intellectual property, with the most highly classified information receiving the greatest protection. We work with legal groups to specify the classification structure and then implement controls on management and distribution of such information to provide the appropriate level of protection. We also partner to respond to suspected or known IP thefts. Suppose an employee loses a laptop storing the designs of future products: a dialogue with IP attorneys is essential to understand the implications and decide how to respond.

Contracts

Almost every contract with a supplier or customer contains a confidentiality provision, which sets expectations about how each party will maintain the confidentiality of the business transaction and any shared confidential information. We partner with the procurement organization as well as the legal group to define and implement these requirements into contracts.

If our company decides to outsource a business application to an external supplier, we'll typically work with the procurement organization and legal team to define these confidentiality and data security expectations, as well as the evidence we'll need to validate that those controls are operating properly. For example, when hiring a company to manage health benefits, we set expectations about how they must protect our employees' personal health information.

Our customers have expectations, too. A computer manufacturer may need to share some IP with us to help us integrate our technology into their product. We need to understand their requirements and ensure that appropriate controls are implemented.

Financial Compliance

In the United States and other countries, public companies are legally required to disclose "material events"—those likely to have significant financial impact that could affect investor decisions, including IT-related incidents. An important aspect of risk governance, therefore, is partnering with legal groups to understand the types of events and specific incidents that must be reported.

Guidance from the US Securities and Exchange Commission specifically discusses the obligation to disclose the impact of cyber attacks, including those that result in IP thefts. Companies are also required to disclose material increases in security spending in response to an attack, even if the attack didn't result in a loss of IP (SEC 2011).

The legal team cannot do this alone because it lacks the security context of the event—the frequency of specific types of attack, the potential impact, and the cost of response. Therefore, the security team must be involved.

In 2010, Google disclosed that it had been breached in the widely publicized Operation Aurora attack. At around the same time, Intel also experienced an incident of similar sophistication. This was before the SEC issued its guidance in 2011, but as I pondered the potential ramifications of a cyber breach one sleepless night, I realized that I should call our SEC legal experts to discuss the incident. Subsequently, we disclosed the incident in our financial report for the first quarter of 2010 (Intel 2010).

Legal Specialists Within Business Groups

At large companies, each business group may have embedded legal experts. We need to work with them for issues directly related to their group. In addition, because of their connections within the group, these legal professionals can be extremely helpful in influencing the group's controls and expectations.

Marketing groups, for example, usually include individuals who want to explore new ways to communicate with users via social media. This appetite for adventure is a good thing; it can benefit the business. But at the same time, we have to ensure that content is adequately protected and includes appropriate privacy protection and statements. If we bring up the issue directly with marketers, we may receive a lukewarm response, as they tend to view any controls as restrictions on their ability to move quickly. But the legal professionals within the marketing group understand the need for controls. So a good way to raise our concerns is to have a conversation with the business group's attorney, who can help persuade others in the group that controls are needed.

At Intel, we implemented a program that reviews all new externally facing online projects and monitors for potential problems (see sidebar). The projects may range from web sites to more sophisticated tools, such as an application that users can download and use in conjunction with external social media sites.

As part of the review, we ask the project group who their legal contacts are so that we can verify that they've received legal approval. We also ask whether trademark and branding teams have reviewed the initiative, which is essential in many cases—especially if the project is planning to register a new web site. Sometimes the answer is no, in which case we can facilitate a dialogue with the trademarks and brands team. This enables the trademark and brand people to manage the risk and helps forge yet another important relationship within the company.

SECURING INTEL'S EXTERNAL ONLINE PRESENCE

Intel's business groups use hundreds of web sites and third-party solutions, including social media platforms, to communicate and conduct business with customers and business partners. Collectively, these externally facing Intel-branded solutions are known as Intel's *external presence*.

Until 2006, these web sites proliferated rapidly in response to business needs, without centralized oversight. Given this growth and following a number of security incidents and the identification of several significant risks, we established the Intel Secure External Presence (ISEP) program to provide appropriate security for Intel's external presence (Leon 2011).

The goals of ISEP, which is part of Intel's information security group, are to protect Intel's information assets and customers against threats such as loss of personal information and malware attacks, and to maintain compliance with laws, regulations, and standards. By achieving these goals, we also help to protect Intel's corporate image.

We help ensure this protection and compliance by reviewing all planned new external presence projects and by monitoring existing Intel-branded web sites. ISEP review and approval is mandatory for new externally facing online projects. We work with Intel business groups to review planned projects before launch, whether they are to be hosted within Intel or by a third party.

The ISEP process includes several key aspects:

We make sure that we receive notification of new projects by working closely with business groups and other stakeholders within Intel. For example, we are notified when business groups request new Internet domain names or seek approval to land a new application in our externally facing IT environment.

For each project, we work with the business group to review details of the planned approach to maintaining security and privacy compliance. We verify that the project includes any required mitigating controls before giving approval.

A key to our success is an overarching governance board, including senior managers from multiple Intel stakeholder groups. This board provides enforcement powers including the ability to shut down web sites for noncompliance.

We have applied the ISEP security review process to hundreds of new projects. In addition, we conduct daily vulnerability scans on all of Intel's externally facing web sites—more than 450—while maintaining a high compliance level with a vulnerability assessment standard based on industry best practices. Overall, ISEP has effectively helped secure externally facing Intel-branded web sites and solutions, resulting in a significant risk reduction for Intel's external presence.

Human Resources

The human resources group is the organization's center of expertise on employee procedures. HR may also include legal specialists who are the organization's experts on employee-related laws. At some organizations, HR is also responsible for other functions, including internal and external communications. Because of this broad charter, the security team may form valuable partnerships with HR in several areas, including employee policies related to appropriate use and protection of information assets, internal communications, and investigations.

Setting Employee Expectations in Security Policies

Employees are part of the security perimeter, as I'll discuss in Chapter 5. Their behavior can have as much impact on security as the technical controls we use—particularly since a growing number of user interactions with the outside world take place on external web sites and networks, and on personal devices such as smartphones.

It is therefore critical to create employee policies that set expectations for secure behavior. If we can influence employees to behave in more secure ways, we can reduce risk for the business overall. However, the security team cannot write these policies without partnering with HR, including HR legal specialists, to ensure that they comply with employment laws and the organization's existing rules. Then, if an employee disregards the policies, we need to work with HR to take disciplinary action.

Careless behavior can have highly damaging consequences. Imagine an IT employee who decides to store some corporate data on a server at his home so that he can more easily work on projects when out of the office. But his home system is open to the Internet, and thus the data may be broadly exposed to anyone worldwide.

The employee's action has created a significant security risk. To explain the potential impact to HR, it may help to use analogies. We could say it's like an engineer taking critical product designs home and showing them to her neighbors. Or a factory employee taking dangerous chemicals home to experiment with them, and creating the danger of an explosion in his garage. If we have a good relationship with HR, we can have this kind of discussion and determine the appropriate consequences for the employee.

Employee Communications

The responsibilities of the employee communications group often include employee training, employee awareness, and internal distribution of other corporate information. This group's expertise can be very useful when we want to communicate security messages to the workforce. The group already has established communication channels and knows how to align messages with corporate style guidelines. A good employee communications group also knows how to present information in ways that engage employees rather than intimidate them.

At Intel, we work extensively with the employee communications group to create engaging security awareness messages, including interactive content that helps encourage secure practices when using social media and the Web.

Investigations

Partnership with HR is also essential in internal investigations. If it's an investigation initiated by HR, they may need our help to identify the information that may have been compromised, the implications, and possible responses. In other cases, we may already be pursuing an investigation and need help from HR legal specialists to access employee information.

Finance

The finance group typically takes the lead in managing risk and controls for the organization overall. Therefore, we need to partner with the finance group to assess the business impact of damage to information assets—a loss of confidentiality, integrity, or availability. We also work together to determine the required controls.

Sarbanes-Oxley Compliance

The corporate finance team usually has overall responsibility for Sarbanes-Oxley (SOX) compliance, so we need to work with them to determine the appropriate controls. We must be able to attest to the financial integrity of our financial statements—to be sure the numbers accurately reflect our financial condition. This requires controls at all levels: within financial business processes, the applications, and the IT infrastructure. We also work with the finance group, as well as legal groups, to determine whether we should categorize specific events as material and report them as required by SOX.

Working with Business Groups

Each sizeable business group is likely to have a group controller or other financial specialist responsible for financial controls. These finance experts can become important partners for the security team.

Because financial specialists focus on risk and controls, the culture among finance specialists has some similarities with the culture of the information risk and security teams. This shared focus can make it easier for us to communicate our concerns, particularly since the impact of information risk is often measured in financial terms. Therefore, the financial specialist can be a key contact point when we need to discuss information risk with business groups.

Sometimes these risk conversations can evolve into productive multi-way partnerships. A recent example: an IT team presented plans for new systems to support one of Intel's new businesses. As we assessed the information risks, we noticed that the plan didn't include fully redundant systems to ensure business continuity. When we asked why, it emerged that the business group hadn't requested redundancy because it would add cost. Revenue from this new business was initially expected to be modest, so the group's budget was limited.

However, when we discussed the revenue projections with the finance specialists who worked on the project, they expected the business to grow rapidly. This growth would also increase the information-related risk because a system failure would have a much bigger impact on revenue. As we discussed the implications, it became clear that it would make more sense to prepare for the anticipated growth by including redundancy from the start. So we suggested that the business group negotiate a higher budget—and that's what happened through a partnership between the business group managers, the information security team, and IT finance and business system specialists. The business group allocated increased funding that allowed IT to implement a redundancy safety net that would protect the growing business.

Internal Audit

Financial groups are often also responsible for internal audit, which typically includes an IT auditing function—a job with considerable potential for overlap with the information security group's role. If the security team and internal auditors duplicate each other's efforts, we'll waste resources and annoy business groups. Imagine if we contact a business manager to say that we need to conduct a risk evaluation of the group's systems. The next day, internal auditors contact the same group and say they're planning to do an audit, which some business managers might perceive to be essentially the same as a risk evaluation. What kind of reception do you think the auditors would receive?

We can minimize the overlap by partnering with internal auditors. This partnership becomes a mechanism for effectively allocating risk management resources. If the information security team has already assessed a system, auditors may be able to increase the efficiency of an audit by leveraging the work that the security team has already performed.

For effective partnership, our work must be thorough, transparent, and well documented so that auditors can see what we have done. We may also swap resources: sometimes security experts may act as guest auditors for specific projects because they have skills that the financial group lacks. The partnership can also be used for valuable dialogue and mutual support. If we're concerned about a system that internal auditors have previously examined, we can ask for their opinion. We'll sleep better knowing that another group of objective, risk-focused specialists has analyzed the system.

Corporate Risk Management

Most large organizations employ people whose job includes purchasing insurance for general business risks, including property and casualty insurance to protect the organization in the event of damage to a data center or another facility. When buying insurance, the corporate risk management team may need information from us about the organization's IT business continuity and disaster recovery plans. Insurers ask for this information in order to set premiums.

Today, the corporate risk management team usually focuses on physical risks. But their scope is rapidly expanding to include IT-related risks as well. Privacy breaches or other compromises can have a major impact on a company's revenue, cost, and brand image. Because of this trend, insurance against cyber risks is a rapidly growing category, and we can expect a growing need to partner with the corporate risk management team to ensure adequate coverage of information risks.

Consider the case of Sony, which suffered a breach of its PlayStation Network—estimated by the company to cost at least USD 200 million (Perlroth 2011)—and then became embroiled in a legal dispute with its insurer, which claimed Sony's insurance policy did not cover cyber risk.

Privacy

Privacy and security are closely linked. However, increasing security doesn't always enhance privacy. In fact, it can have the opposite effect. Unfettered monitoring of information and activities can increase security but intrude on personal privacy.

This creates inherent tension between security and privacy interests. This tension is apparent at a national level in the way that privacy advocates respond to the use of surveillance and data mining. Government security organizations may feel that they protect data extremely well, but privacy advocates still object to the fact that information is collected and the way it is used.

Similar concerns apply at the enterprise level. We need to carefully manage the relationship between security and privacy, ensuring that we apply the appropriate level of controls to protect information without infringing on personal privacy.

The structure of this relationship varies between organizations. At Intel, the information risk group includes a privacy team that reports to the CISO. At other organizations, privacy is the responsibility of a separate group headed by a chief privacy officer who is the CISO's peer. This arrangement necessitates careful management of the relationship between security and privacy teams to manage tension, align policies, and control breaches. In organizations with this structure, the security team sometimes complains that the privacy team is "getting in their way"—which usually means that the security team wants to collect specific information and the privacy team objects.

Regardless of the organizational structure, it is the security team that is logically responsible for implementing IT controls. Laws define privacy rights; the organization's interpretation of those laws drives compliance requirements. It is the security team's responsibility to determine how to implement controls to support those requirements.

Corporate Security

The corporate security team focuses on physical security concerns—ranging from door locks and guards to break-ins, fires, and natural disasters. By partnering with this team, we can make sure we're aligned on protection of key information assets. It wouldn't make sense to implement sophisticated data-protection tools on the servers in the data center—and then leave the data center doors unlocked.

We also need to coordinate on other issues, including incidents that involve law enforcement. Not so long ago, assaults and harassment were almost always physical incidents handled by corporate security and the police. Today, there's a much bigger overlap with information security. More crime is moving online, and we may encounter other problems, such as cyber bullying. Because of these trends, we may need to help assess the impact and drive the response.

Business Group Managers

Each business group has its own processes and applications—whether it's a product-focused unit responsible for generating revenue or an internal group managing finance or human resources. The information security team needs to partner with each group to implement security controls that protect the group's applications and information.

Direct relationships with business group managers and any risk management specialists within their groups, are invaluable for strategic and tactical reasons. By working closely with business managers, we can better understand their security priorities. As the business acumen of our information security team increases, we can better fulfill our "protect to enable" mission by focusing on controls that improve security without impeding the business.

By working with business groups, we can also leverage their strengths. Business group managers can help drive decision-making and incident response. They can also help improve security by setting the "tone at the top"—publicly setting expectations for their employees' security behavior. Suppose we notice that an increasing number of the employees at a specific facility are experiencing laptop thefts. We discuss the trend with the general manager and explain that we want to increase employees' awareness with messages about how to prevent theft. The business manager may offer to help by bringing up the topic at a site meeting or otherwise directly communicating with employees. This management request may exert a more powerful influence on employee behavior than messages sent by the security group.

HOW INTEL IT RESPONDS TO EMERGENCIES

Defining a clear IT incident response process is an essential aspect of IT governance. Over time, Intel IT has developed a clearly defined crisis management process for responding to emergencies and other significant incidents that affect IT infrastructure or services (Fleming and Tomizawa 2012). The goal of the process is to prevent material impact to Intel and its employees.

Incidents that may trigger the process include cyber events and other information security incidents; physical incidents such as fires, leaks, and major outages that affect IT systems; and major disease outbreaks. We developed the process using incident management principles based on the US Federal Emergency Management Agency's response to disasters.

Once initiated, the Intel IT Emergency Response Process (ITERP) operates with a command-and-control structure, led by an incident commander who has overriding authority to make decisions across IT for the duration of the emergency. The structure consists of a virtual organization staffed on a volunteer basis by people from every discipline within IT. When an incident occurs, all team members perform their response roles instead of their normal duties until all issues are resolved.

Following an incident, we quickly identify the state of critical business processes that must continue during the crisis. We determine the current status of the key steps in our product cycle: design, build, order, ship, pay, and close. We assess the physical state of the infrastructure. We analyze the legal and other impacts if intellectual property or personal information is compromised. Decisions about response and remediation are driven by the incident commander and determined by business priorities.

The ITERP team has proved to be an essential component of the successful resolution of every crisis management, coordination, control, and communication activity in IT for the past 11 years.

Conclusion

Information risk has become a major concern for the entire organization. Managing information risk therefore requires a clear governance structure that enables the organization to make the right security decisions quickly and effectively.

Think about how your own organization manages information risk. Do you develop strategies in close collaboration with business groups? Do you feel that you communicate well enough with every group to understand their priorities and implement controls that reflect them? Have you clearly defined all the processes required to respond to a major breach or denial-of-service attack? If you answered "no" to any of these questions, you may need to improve your information risk governance.

Effective governance relies on partnerships between the information security team and other internal groups across practically every part of organization. In this chapter, I've described some of the most important partnerships and the value we can derive from them.

To develop these partnerships, CISOs need more than just technical skills. We need to communicate in terms business people understand and build relationships that enable us to influence people at all levels across the organization. As the scope of information security expands, we also need extensive management and leadership skills, both to operate at an executive level and to inspire our security team. I'll discuss these skills in detail in Chapter 9.

CHAPTER 4

■ ■ ■

External Partnerships

The Power of Sharing Information

Chance favors the connected mind.

—Steven Johnson

After spending a day at a conference, I was having dinner with a dozen or so peers when a debate began about the dangers and benefits of sharing security information with other companies. One person turned to me and asked if I had information about a specific new threat, would I share it with him.

"You bet," I said.

"But what if I was your competitor—would you still share?" he asked.

"Our companies might compete for business," I replied, "but in the security arena, my real competitors are the malicious actors who want to harm my company's information systems. Those are my competitors, and they're your competitors, too."

As soon as I'd said this, several people at the table agreed. This agreement was gratifying—and not just because I felt that I had support for my views. The bigger implication was that my peers saw the value of sharing information outside their companies.

This hasn't always been the case. In fact, many organizations still frown on the idea of sharing security information externally, and some have policies that forbid it.

There are two primary reasons why organizations are afraid to share. First, they have concerns about the legal implications of revealing security information. A second, related concern is the public-relations aspect. Both of these fears have a valid basis. Information security has become an enterprise risk management issue of board-level interest because of the potential effects. Information leaks revealing potential intrusions and data breaches can have legal consequences: the organization may be required to report the problems in order to comply with financial and privacy regulations, for example. If security issues become public, they may also damage the way the organization is perceived by customers and by the business community, potentially affecting a company's profitability and its stock price.

Despite these concerns, I believe that it is becoming increasingly important to partner with other organizations to share information about security-related issues such as threats and best practices. As I'll explain in this chapter, sharing security information can provide considerable benefits in managing the risk of moving into new business relationships and adopting new technologies. We just need to find ways to reduce the risk of sharing. The solution lies in creating trusted information-sharing relationships with other organizations. The more we trust the relationship, the more sensitive the information that can be shared.

The need to share security information is being driven by rapidly changing business, technology, and threat landscapes. Increasingly, companies are collaborating with a broad variety of business partners. We share business information, and often we also use the same information technology. As we do so, we also share risks. Understanding the risks faced by our partners, and the way they manage those risks, can help us protect our own organizations.

Looking more broadly across the technology landscape, all systems and devices are to some extent connected—whether they are owned by enterprises, individuals, or service providers. Almost every aspect of society depends on a worldwide, rapidly evolving, highly complex network of devices and services. This provides the central nervous system that supports innovation, economic development, and social interaction worldwide. But because we are all inherently interconnected, we share common risks. The threat landscape is dynamic, global, and increasingly complex. Threats may originate in any country and then spread rapidly across national and enterprise boundaries, causing extensive damage to organizations and individuals worldwide.

Because threats spread so quickly and the threat landscape is so complex, it is hard for any single organization to gain a clear view of all potential vulnerabilities, threats, and attacks. External partnerships can help. They provide additional intelligence that we can use to improve our own security posture. By exchanging information with other organizations, we gain what I call *outsight*, or a better understanding of what happens outside our own environment. We learn about new threats before they hit us directly. We see how other organizations are managing those threats. We learn about best practices for managing security operations. Using the information we gather from external relationships, we can increase the organization's ability to sense, interpret, and act on risk.

The Value of External Partnerships

Sharing security-related information can require initiative and courage. The idea of sharing information externally may run counter to the culture of the organization overall, including the culture within the security group. Organizations may view security information as proprietary and confidential, like intellectual property. Many still have policies against sharing information.

It's true that much security information is sensitive, and sharing it can introduce risks. Because of this, we need to be careful about what we share and with whom.

But think about the broader context of how organizations are increasingly sharing information. Most organizations have already recognized they need to share sensitive business information with partners in order to develop, manufacture, and market new products. Collaboration with other companies is becoming an integral part of many other business processes, too. As organizations share information, they benefit from their partners' insights and expertise. As noted by Steven Johnson, author of *Where Good Ideas Come From: The Natural History of Innovation* (Riverhead Books, 2010), many of the best ideas have emerged not through the inspiration of a single mind, but through the exchange of ideas. "You have half of an idea, somebody else has the other half, and if you're in the right environment, they turn into something larger than the sum of their parts," Johnson said in a speech at the 2010 TEDGlobal conference (Johnson 2010). "We often talk about the value of protecting intellectual property—building barricades, having secretive R&D labs, patenting everything that we have, so that those ideas will remain valuable . . . but I think there's a case to be made that we should spend at least as much time, if not more, valuing the premise of connecting ideas and not just protecting them."

I believe that there's similar value in sharing security information. As we collaborate with business partners, we need to understand the threats to their environment, and how they manage risk, in order to determine what we need to do to protect our own organizations. Each partner in a value chain needs to protect information to a level that is adequate to protect the other partners; the weakest link in the chain can impact everyone. Note that throughout this chapter, I use the terms "partner" and "partnership" in the colloquial sense, not to imply any specific type of formal legal relationship.

There are many other examples of how sharing information can benefit all organizations involved. If we are entering new markets through business partnerships, we need to understand the nature of the threats in those markets from the companies currently operating there. The same logic applies to using new technologies. Organizations are extending their environment to customers and becoming suppliers of mobile apps and web services in the process. As they do, they can learn from other companies' experience how to manage the risks. Companies are increasingly sharing cloud capacity or other data-center infrastructure supplied by external providers, and can all benefit by sharing feedback with the provider about risks within the environment.

Despite these trends, some organizations still have policies stipulating that employees shouldn't share internal information about risks and threats with anyone outside the company. This is sometimes the case even when the same organization willingly shares other IT-related information such as helpdesk or e-mail management best practices.

Without wishing to discount the real fears driving these policies, the value of sharing information often outweighs the risk of doing so. Let's imagine that a CISO learns of a new threat affecting companies in his industry sector. He shares information about the threat with a peer at another company and, by doing so, gains insight that helps the organization mitigate an attack that has caused massive damage at other companies. By sharing information against company policy, the CISO took a personal risk. Yet by doing so, he averted the bigger risk of business disruption and damage to the organization's reputation.

Failure to share information with others introduces its own risks. If we don't share with peers, they won't share with us, so we won't benefit from their information and insights. I've seen cases in which information security professionals wanted to participate in communities, but weren't allowed by their companies to share any internal security-related information. So they attended meetings but couldn't contribute. Ultimately, their peers wouldn't tolerate a situation in which these people were receiving information but giving nothing in return, and they were effectively voted off the island.

External Partnerships: Types and Tiers

Much of the publicity about information-sharing initiatives has focused on public-private partnerships related to critical infrastructure and national security. However, there are many other types of formal and informal external information-sharing relationships, including 1:1 partnerships and groups comprised solely of private-sector organizations.

External partnerships are most often used to share information about specific threats and best security practices. But some partnerships focus on other types of information. For example, security specialists within the high-tech sector share information in order to develop security standards, which are then implemented in various products.

Much of this security information is sensitive. Because of this, we need to be able to trust that the partners with whom we share information will treat it appropriately. The more sensitive the information, the greater the level of trust required. In general, the level of trust can be higher in relationships with fewer people, allowing more-sensitive information to be shared. As the number of people increases, there's a greater chance that information will leak, so the level of trust tends to decrease and only less-sensitive information is shared.

Relationships therefore naturally tend to fall into a tiered pyramid model, as shown in Figure 4-1 and described further in Table 4-1 (Willis 2012). At the top of the pyramid are the most-trusted relationships with the fewest partners—1:1 partnerships between two individuals at different organizations, or between two security teams.

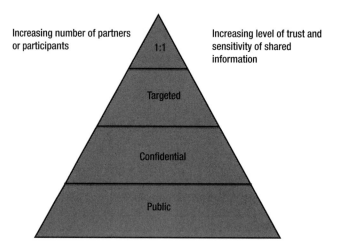

Figure 4-1. *Tiered pyramid model for trusted information-sharing partnerships and communities (Adapted from Willis 2012). Source: Intel Corporation, 2012*

Table 4-1. Characteristics of Security Information-Sharing Partnerships and Communities (Adapted from Willis 2012)

Tier	Community Structure	Typical Number of Partners	Example Partnership/ Community	Example Goal	Trust Framework
1:1 Partnerships	Direct communication between CISOs at two organizations, or between their teams	2	Any two organizations who choose to share information	To mitigate shared threats by exchanging information with a business partner more quickly and in greater detail than would be possible within a larger group	Personal trust and existing business relationships
Targeted	A relatively small number of critical information infrastructure owners and operators sharing information to protect the infrastructure. Also includes key security ecosystem influencers, such as large security service providers or vendors.	Up to about 15	Information Sharing and Analysis Centers (ISACs)	To prevent advanced persistent threats (APT) within the industrial base by sharing APT signature information	Strong information-sharing frameworks, such as national security clearances and nondisclosure agreements, are required. Trusted sharing mechanisms, such as encrypted web portals with multifactor authentication, are also required.

(continued)

47

Table 4-1. (continued)

Tier	Community Structure	Typical Number of Partners	Example Partnership/ Community	Example Goal	Trust Framework
Confidential	Communities that represent industry sectors or other groupings, such as the banking sector and Internet service providers (ISPs); regional forums	Up to about 50	BITS (financial services Industry) Bay Area CSO Council (regional) Regional CSO Summits	To enable members to protect against common threats and vulnerabilities affecting their industries. For example, ISPs might share the command and control Internet addresses that botnets use.	Communities typically use trust frameworks such as nondisclosure agreements or memoranda of understanding
Public	A broad range of communities that represent all user categories, including consumers, small- and medium-sized businesses, and industry in general	More than 50	Forum for Incident Response and Security Teams (FIRST) National Cyber Security Alliance	To share best practices or informational bulletins about widely known threats and vulnerabilities that affect a large cross-section of users	Trust frameworks are not necessary; communities typically distribute information broadly through mechanisms such as e-mail distribution lists or public web sites.

Information-sharing relationships between more than two partners are often referred to as communities. Because more people are involved, a legal or peer-enforced agreement is usually needed to define the level of trust and confidentiality expected among community members.

The two middle tiers of the pyramid include groups with intermediate levels of trust, sharing information with varying levels of sensitivity. The *Targeted tier* typically consists of public-private partnerships aimed at protecting critical infrastructure. The *Confidential tier* includes many private-sector communities, including regional communities and those focused on specific industry sectors.

At the bottom of the pyramid is the *Public tier*, comprised of the largest communities with the lowest level of trust. At this level, information is often public and may be broadcast via the Internet. This tier might include groups that develop educational information about threats for public distribution, or CISOs who share their insights via public webcasts.

How can you get involved in information-sharing partnerships? One good method is to start by participating in communities in the Public tier, where the information shared has a relatively low level of sensitivity and therefore involves little risk. In these communities, you're likely to meet peers with whom you can begin to engage in 1:1 partnerships. As you become more knowledgeable about the communities that reflect your organization's key interests, you may then become involved in communities in the middle tiers of the pyramid, where more confidential information is exchanged. At Intel's Information Risk and Security group, we participate in partnerships in all the tiers of the pyramid.

1:1 Partnerships

In my experience, 1:1 partnerships are some of the most valuable security relationships. They may be formal or informal, established at a corporate level or between individuals.

As I explained, a key advantage of a trusted 1:1 partnership is that we can more safely share highly confidential information. We can often create a stronger bond with a single individual than with a larger group. As a result, the shared information often has a depth and richness that's lacking in information shared within larger communities.

Another advantage is speed. Communication is often fastest in 1:1 partnerships, partly due to logistics. It's much easier to set up a meeting between two people than it is to organize a meeting with a dozen people. To exchange information about the latest developments, a CISO may be able to simply pick up the phone and have a conversation with his or her peer. Quickly sharing information enables a faster response to threats—and in the security arena, timeliness is often critical.

Here's an example showing how 1:1 partnerships can develop and benefit both partners. Through my participation in a larger security community, I got to know the CISO at a fast-growing e-commerce company whose customers were primarily consumers. We both would contact each other periodically for advice and information as we puzzled over the latest security challenges. Over time, these conversations evolved into open dialogues about best practices and benchmarking.

The relationship eventually evolved to a point where we both realized we could learn a great deal more by bringing our teams together in a face-to-face meeting. The resulting half-day meeting proved incredibly valuable to both teams. Our team was able to provide insights and experiences about managing security in a large, complex enterprise environment. This was helpful to the security team at the fast-growing e-commerce company, which was in the process of building an enterprise environment to support its fast-growing business. In return, the team at the e-commerce company was able to share the security challenges and experiences of operating a large consumer business with millions of online customers. This was extremely valuable to us at Intel, because we were in the process of expanding our external online presence and were beginning to encounter some of the same challenges.

The partnership thus expanded from ad hoc conversations to a productive relationship between teams sharing experiences and best practices at multiple levels. It's hard to imagine that this extensive information exchange could have occurred within a larger community.

Another example: I met the CISO of a large manufacturing company at an industry event, and we stayed in touch through occasional e-mails. Then, during a period of especially large-scale industry attacks, our communications suddenly became much more frequent and detailed. It was extremely valuable to be able to pick up the phone and simply call a peer to share the latest knowledge about the attacks and responses.

As Intel's CISO, I have frequent 1:1 meetings with peers at other companies, sometimes as often as several times a week. These meetings can serve several purposes. Recently, I met with a team from a key supplier to discuss our strategy for securing employees' personal (bring-your-own) devices. I shared our best practices with this team, and during the question-and-answer discussion, team members also provided information about how they were addressing the same problem. The meeting served as a helpful benchmarking exercise for all of us.

At the same time, the discussion clearly demonstrated each company's commitment to protecting its partner's business information. It showed the depth of each company's strategy for protecting information—revealing a commitment that extended far beyond the desire to comply with contract confidentiality clauses. I felt more confident that if a security issue ever arose, I could talk directly to my counterparts at the supplier company because their commitment to protecting information would enable a productive approach to resolving problems.

Communities

Participating in larger communities may not provide information that's quite as rich and deep as the information you'd obtain from a 1:1 partnership with a peer. But communities provide value in other ways.

Because they contain more people, communities provide breadth and diversity of perspective that help us make balanced risk decisions. With a larger number of participants, there's a better chance that one of them will have developed a solution to a problem, or provide valuable new information about an industry attack.

Some communities focus on sharing threat-related information; others on benchmarking and best practices, influencing legislation, developing security standards, or public education.

Communities can also present great networking opportunities. Through participation in communities, I've met several people with whom I've subsequently developed closer 1:1 partnerships.

Community Characteristics

Like all groups, communities require a structure and set of ground rules to be effective. Successful communities typically have the following characteristics:

- *Clear goals.* The community shares clearly defined common goals that benefit members, such as mitigating an industry-wide threat. A community may have several goals.

- *A strong framework of trust, such as a legal or peer-enforced agreement, that addresses risks related to information sharing among community members.* For example, the Industry Consortium for the Advancement of Security on the Internet (ICASI) has a strong multilateral nondisclosure agreement, while other communities, such as the Bay Area CSO Council, rely on a peer-enforced trust framework.

- *Trusted communications channels.* Members can safely contribute and access shared information using an effective trusted communications channel or mechanism, such as a secure web site. These channels are not always electronic; some regional groups conduct face-to-face meetings to further reduce the risk of compromise.

An organization is most likely to benefit from joining communities if those communities align with the organization's security goals. This means it's important to first clearly define those organizational security goals. To do this, some organizations have found it helpful to use a structured approach—they can more clearly categorize their goals by mapping them to a standard risk management model, such as the "defense in depth" model. Once an organization clearly understands its own security goals, it can identify communities whose objectives align with these goals.

Because there is such a diverse range of organizations, security threats, and goals, it is unlikely that any single information-sharing community structure meets all the needs of a large organization. For example, a company might participate in one community for benchmarking and another to tackle industry-specific threats.

Information-sharing communities thrive only when the participating organizations feel they're receiving valuable information, creating incentives to continue to share information with others.

What constitutes valuable information? A common definition is that information should be timely and specific, relevant to participants' concerns, and providing a suitable level of detail while protecting individual privacy (ENISA 2010). In practice, "valuable" usually means the information helps you achieve your security goals, whether those goals are long-term and strategic, or short-term and operational. Information useful for strategic goals might include an early warning that attackers are expected to target a specific industry. This helps members of the community plan their defenses. Information useful for operational goals typically includes more specific details, such as an attack signature. This helps organizations more quickly identify an attack and respond when it occurs.

As shown in Figure 4-1 and Table 4-1 (the Targeted tier), some communities consist of government agencies working alongside industry in what are usually known as public-private partnerships (PPPs). These PPPs can be particularly important for protecting critical information infrastructure. Internationally and within many nations, this infrastructure is largely owned and operated by the private sector, including carriers and network service providers. Sharing information about threats and attacks among public and private agencies therefore can help ensure security and resiliency of this infrastructure. Because the shared information is highly sensitive, these PPPs usually have strong trust frameworks including national security clearances.

Other communities primarily include private-sector organizations. Members of an industry may get together to share best practices, helping to reduce risk for each company while enhancing the industry's reputation overall.

Some communities are regional, aimed at security professionals from private and public-sector organizations located within a specific area. These regional communities offer the advantage of convenience. It takes less time, effort, and expense to attend a regional event, which makes participation more attractive.

Examples of regional groups and forums include the San Francisco Bay Area CSO Council, described shortly. Other useful regional events include the CISO Executive Summits organized by Evanta. These are invitation-only gatherings at which CISOs and other industry experts share insights and information about a wide range of areas, including legal, policy, and security issues.

New communities arise frequently. A community may form in response to a specific threat because companies are strongly motivated to share information about the threat in order to develop effective defenses. For example, the Conficker Work Group was formed specifically to address the risk posed by the Conficker worm.

Community Goals

Communities may focus on narrowly defined goals, such as mitigating a specific threat, or they may have broader information-sharing goals, such as benchmarking security techniques. A single community may pursue several goals. The most well-known types of goal are sharing information about threats (to help member organizations mitigate those threats) and sharing best practices (to improve efficiency). I'll describe the main categories of information-sharing goals next.

Sharing Information About Threats and Vulnerabilities

Perhaps the best-known function of communities is to provide a trusted mechanism for sharing information about threats and vulnerabilities. Members of the community can use this information to improve their tactical and strategic situational awareness.

I'm often asked by peers how I measure the value of the information obtained from external partnerships. A key metric is whether the early threat information has helped enable us to reduce risk. A single piece of information might make participation worthwhile if it helps us better mitigate risk and protect the company.

Information from the community can also be useful for corroborating evidence that we've already identified internally. If we observe a potential new threat within our environment, we may not feel that we have enough evidence to justify taking action. But we can often discuss the issue within a community. If others are experiencing the same problem, we can be more confident that it's a real issue. This gives us enough reason to act.

Some examples of communities that share threat information include:

- *Bay Area CSO Council.* This is a regional community that focuses on improving the sharing of intelligence and best practices among CISOs in the San Francisco Bay Area. The Council serves as a vehicle for CISOs to safely and securely share their attack experiences. Members may share artifacts, such as attack signatures, that they can then build into their organizations' detection and defense mechanisms (Jackson Higgins 2010). The forum uses a peer-enforced trust model rather than a formal legal framework. The group also creates subgroups to work on more highly classified information.

- *Information Sharing and Analysis Centers (ISACs).* ISACs are trusted industry-specific communities established by owners and operators of critical infrastructure resources. ISACs exist for a number of industry sectors, including communications, electrical utility, health, and public transit. Services provided by ISACs include risk mitigation, incident response, and alert and information sharing. Intel is a member of the IT sector ISAC (IT-ISAC), which focuses on sharing cyber situational awareness information between IT industry members in the United States. The IT-ISAC has a legal framework of trust characterized by a memorandum of understanding among members.

Sharing Best Practices and Benchmarking

Many communities also serve as a forum for exchanging best practices and for benchmarking operations. By sharing security best practices, we may be able to increase the efficiency and effectiveness of our own operations.

Tapping into the expertise of others can help us avoid reinventing the wheel. A typical example: A CISO is trying to create a bring-your-own device policy for her own organization. So she sends a message to community members and receives detailed advice from others who have already been through the process. This gives the CISO a head start in creating a policy that meets her organization's needs.

Besides enabling informal exchanges, communities may also operate formal benchmarking exercises. One of the best-known examples is the Information Risk Executive Council, which conducts studies and generates reports that compare companies in a variety of areas, from user security awareness to controls maturity (Corporate Executive Board 2012). Benchmarking information generated by communities can also be useful for demonstrating the efficiency of security operations to other internal groups within your organization, such as an audit committee.

Some benchmarking information is sensitive and closely held because organizations feel that it could reveal too much information about their security operations. Other information is more general and is sometimes publicly available, such as the webinars and presentations published online by Intel and others. Even this general benchmarking information may yield risk insights. Observing what other companies are focusing on, and how they are allocating resources, can help security professionals think about how they need to manage risk within their own organizations.

One of the most established communities is the Forum for Incident Response and Security Teams (FIRST). This international group focuses on sharing best practices among computer security incident response teams. Trust relationships are peer-enforced. The group publishes a series of detailed best-practices guides and other documents for public use. Other activities involve the exchange of information for cooperative incident management.

BENCHMARKING: WHO SHOULD YOU COMPARE YOURSELF WITH?

Many years ago, I was asked to manage Intel's first major IT benchmarking activity. It was a big task that entailed analyzing cost, quality, and other aspects of operations across our entire IT environment.

One of the first challenges was determining which organizations we should benchmark ourselves against. At the time, the conventional wisdom at most organizations, including Intel, was that you should compare yourself with similar businesses. The logic was that because these businesses were the most directly comparable, this approach would yield the most meaningful results. So the expectation was that I'd benchmark our operations against a collection of other big high-tech companies.

But I didn't want to benchmark our operations against only high-tech companies. Instead, I wanted to benchmark against a broad base of companies in industries such as retail, banking, manufacturing, consumer goods, and utilities.

The time came to present my selection of peer groups in a meeting with senior IT management. By this time, I'd already started the benchmarking process, and as I described the diversity of the companies included in the benchmark comparison, I could sense the atmosphere becoming increasingly hostile. Practically everyone felt that my approach was completely wrong. In fact, if there had been rotten tomatoes in the room, a few people would have been throwing them at me.

So I asked for a moment of quiet so that I could explain. "If we were an airline that wanted to benchmark operations, who would we compare ourselves with?" I asked. Several people said they'd benchmark against other airlines.

"What do you think we would learn from that comparison?" I continued. "My guess is not much. We'd all have grown up in the same industry, and we'd probably have similar business processes. Many of our employees would have worked for the other companies and vice versa, so they'd probably implement similar practices. We might learn about minor efficiency improvements, but I wouldn't expect any breakthroughs.

"If I really wanted to dramatically improve the way I manage airline gate operations, I'd benchmark against a Formula 1 pit crew. Those crews can service a car and get it back on the road in 20 seconds or less. I'd think about what we could learn from studying their processes, their technologies, and their ability to communicate and organize, and I'd try to figure out which aspects could cross over into airline data operations. If we want to make dramatic improvements, we need to look at people who operate in an extreme operational environment—not at other airlines."

I'm happy to say that the managers in the room recognized that there might be value in the approach I was suggesting, even if many of them still disagreed with it. Ultimately, benchmarking against companies in a broad range of industries did help us achieve some dramatic improvements, and I received an internal award for the initiative. The lesson is that sometimes we can learn more by looking outside a narrowly defined, traditional peer group. People in the same industry may be facing the same problems as we are and dealing with them the same way. For a fresh perspective, it can be worth looking farther afield.

Influencing Regulations and Standards

All of us operate within an increasingly complex regulatory environment, and we're all affected by evolving technology standards.

It's important to stay abreast of legislative developments. That can be a difficult and time-consuming job for any single organization, and so it may be helpful to become involved in a community whose goals include tracking regulatory activity.

In addition, communities can sometimes help influence public policy more effectively than a single organization can do alone. There's strength in numbers, and communities often include some of the biggest companies in an industry.

An example of a community that focuses on policy is BITS (www.bits.org), the technology policy division of The Financial Services Roundtable, which represents 100 of the largest integrated providers of consumer financial services. Members of BITS cooperate on issues such as critical infrastructure protection, fraud prevention, and the safety of financial services. The organization works to influence public policy by communicating with public agencies. It also publishes reports for use across the industry, including a financial services security assessment. Thus, communities that focus on policy may help all participating companies and the reputation of the industry overall.

Businesses who offer services in multiple countries have a particular interest in the international regulatory environment. These include multinationals, of course, which are directly affected by the complex web of regulations at international, national, and local levels.

However, these regulations affect a surprisingly large number of other companies, too—including many that don't have employees or facilities physically located in other countries. Today, almost any business with a web-based service consumed in multiple countries is effectively operating in a multinational environment. Regulations in those countries have impacts that stretch beyond geographical boundaries. For example, regional and local regulations such as the California data breach bill (SB1386) and European privacy guidelines require compliance by any company that stores information about residents of those areas, no matter where the company is located.

Corporate Citizenship

At many companies, including Intel, a large number of employees volunteer in ways that benefit their neighborhood or a wide variety of worthy causes. Businesses often provide support to help employees do this. There's a growing trend to leverage the organization's talent and expertise in volunteer corporate citizenship initiatives that are more closely related to the organization's goals and employees' technical expertise. Examples might include offering expert security advice to nonprofits or helping security initiatives in other countries.

Security-related corporate citizenship initiatives include the National Cyber Security Alliance, whose mission is to educate and empower society to use the Internet safely and securely (see staysafeonline.org). The sponsors of the alliance include large high-tech companies such as Intel. Senior managers at those companies also are among the directors of the organization.

Conclusion

The knowledge we acquire via external partnerships can help us protect our own organizations. The security landscape has become increasingly complex and dynamic, and it's difficult to track and manage the risks without help from others. Sharing security information is also becoming more important as organizations increasingly collaborate with business partners and adopt new technologies. Understanding the risks faced by our partners, and the way they manage those risks, can help us protect our own organizations. As businesses move into new markets and use technology in new ways, we need to understand our biggest exposures and how to allocate resources most effectively to minimize business risk. Therefore, sharing information can help businesses remain competitive and successful.

Organizations have often been reluctant to share security information, but if we want help from other people, we have to be prepared to share information ourselves. By carefully using trusted partnerships that align with our security goals, we can increase the organization's ability to sense, interpret, and act on risk.

CHAPTER 5

■ ■ ■

People Are the Perimeter

A few years ago, one of our senior managers began bringing his corporate laptop into the cafeteria at lunchtime. Typically, he'd find an empty table, set down the laptop, and then walk out of sight to get his lunch. As he perused the salads and main courses, made selections, and paid for his food, his laptop sat unattended in plain view of hundreds of people using the large cafeteria.

My security team noticed the neglected laptop and pointed it out to me. I discussed the issue with the manager a few times, but he continued leaving the laptop unattended. So eventually, I began taking the laptop and leaving my business card in its place.

Not surprisingly, the manager became somewhat annoyed. "Nobody's going to steal the laptop because there are all these people around," he said.

"Okay," I responded. "I'll never take your laptop or complain again on one condition. If you really trust everybody here, you'll take off your wedding ring and leave it on top of the laptop. If you do that, you'll never hear from me again."

He thought about this for a while. Then he said, "You made your point." And he never again left the laptop unattended.

The Shifting Perimeter

This incident helped crystallize in my mind a new perspective about how we should approach information security. It occurred soon after we transitioned from desktop to laptop computers within Intel, and it demonstrated how each person's daily decisions can affect the risk dynamics of the company overall.

The traditional enterprise security paradigm, often expressed in castle-and-drawbridge terms, described a wall of technology that isolated and completely protected the workers behind it. To protect our people and information assets, we focused our efforts on fortifying the network perimeter and the physical perimeter of our buildings.

Today, however, a growing number of user interactions with the outside world bypass the physical and network perimeters and the security controls these perimeters offer. They take place on external web sites and social networks, on laptops in coffee shops and homes, and on personal devices such as smartphones. The laptop left unattended in the cafeteria was clearly inside the physical perimeter, but the corporate information it contained was still potentially at risk due to the manager's actions.

This changing environment doesn't mean the security perimeter has vanished. Instead, it has shifted to the user. People have become part of the perimeter. Every day, users make decisions that can have as much impact on security as the technical controls we use. Do I leave my computer unattended or not? Do I post this information online or not? Do I install this software on my device? Do I report this suspicious-looking e-mail? When I'm in a coffee shop, do I connect to the corporate infrastructure via a secure virtual private network, or do I engage directly over the Internet?

We could view each of these decisions purely in terms of the potential for increased risk. However, there's also a positive side. If users become more aware of security and make better decisions, they can strengthen the organization's defenses by helping identify threats and prevent impact.

Therefore, as information security professionals, we are in the behavior modification business. Our goals include creating a more security-conscious workforce so that users are more aware of threats and vulnerabilities and make better security decisions. Furthermore, we need to influence employees' behavior both within the workplace and when they are home or traveling.

If the manager was comfortable leaving his laptop unattended in our cafeteria, would he also leave it unattended at the local coffee shop? At the airport? Or somewhere else where the risk of loss was even greater? My belief is he probably would. When trying to influence this person's behavior, I wanted to achieve more than a level of compliance. I wanted to initiate a feeling of commitment.

The term *compliant behavior* implies making the minimum effort necessary to achieve good performance to a predefined standard. It's like checking boxes on a list of security compliance items. Ultimately, employees feel they are being compelled to follow someone else's list of instructions. Because of this, compliance requires supervision and policing, and employees may sometimes engage in lengthy recreational complaining. If employees are simply following a checklist, what happens when they encounter a situation that's not on the list? They stop and await further instructions, or perhaps they are even unaware of the threat or ignore it.

In contrast, committed behavior is intrinsically motivated and self-directed. Being committed implies that people are emotionally impelled to invest in security—they take responsibility and ownership. When people feel committed, they tend to deliver above and beyond the bare minimum. Rather than simply following a predefined list of instructions, they are empowered to make decisions and judgment calls in real time, with a focus on how their actions affect others as well as themselves.

If we can create this sense of commitment in our users, we can implement security not as a wall but as a collective security force that permeates the entire organization. Individually and as a group, every person in the corporation uses their skills in security to protect the organization, handling known attacks today as well as quickly adapting to new threats tomorrow.

When I needed to influence the manager's behavior, I looked for a way to establish this level of commitment. I sought to change the way he felt about the laptop, and to do this I tapped into his emotional connection to his wedding ring.

Creating a culture of self-motivated commitment rather than compliance can make a big difference, as shown in studies by management guru Dov Seidman. His group looked at behavioral differences between businesses with a culture of self-governance, in which an organization's purpose and values inform employee decision-making and behavior, and those with a culture of blind obedience based on command-and-control and coercion. Organizations based on self-governance experienced three times more employee loyalty and half as many incidents of misconduct, compared with organizations based on blind obedience (Seidman 2011).

The implications for enterprise security are clear. As the boundaries between personal and corporate computing dissolve, employees may be accessing information from any location, on any device. If users behave in an insecure way while they are in the office, it's likely they will also exhibit insecure behavior when they're elsewhere. Conversely, if we can create a feeling of commitment that causes them to own responsibility for security, there's a better chance they will behave more securely both within the workplace and when they are outside our physical perimeter. This change in behavior improves the security of the device they are using, the information they are accessing, their personal lives, and the enterprise.

Examining the Risks

Before discussing ways that we can modify user behavior, I'd like to briefly mention an example of what can happen if we don't influence the ways that users think and act.

As an experiment, the US Department of Homeland Security secretly dropped disks and thumb drives in the parking lots of government and private contractors' buildings. Their goal was to see whether people would pick them up and plug them into their computers. As reported by Bloomberg News (Edwards et al. 2011), up to 60 percent of the people who picked up the items inserted them into their office computers. That number rose to 90 percent if the item included an official-looking logo. Clearly, the security behavior of employees at these facilities left quite a bit to be desired.

If that's what happens with technologies that have been around for decades, think about what can happen with newer, more sophisticated exploits. Today, threats may arrive in the form of carefully crafted personalized communications designed to win the trust of targeted users. These users then unwittingly provide access to the information the attackers want.

Let's say a company is looking to hire a credit analyst with a very specific set of skills. Attackers notice this and apply online, using a résumé that lists the exact skills required for the job, and contains the terms the company's résumé-scanning software is likely to be looking for. Suitably impressed, the company's human-resources specialists forward the application to the company's credit-department manager, who has access to all the systems storing customer financial data. The manager trusts this communication because it's sent from another department within the same company. So she clicks on the link to the résumé. Unfortunately, that action triggers the execution of malicious code. The human-resources team effectively acted as an infection agent, ensuring the attack reached its real target.

Careless behavior outside the enterprise can create other risks. In a blog post, software engineer Gary LosHuertos (2010) described how, while sitting in a café, he used a freely available packet-sniffing tool to obtain the social media identities of around 40 people who were using the café's Wi-Fi network. Some of these people remained logged into the social media site even after he sent them messages informing them that he had just collected their login information. As he explained, a compromised account doesn't just provide access to the social media site; it can also be used to perform social engineering attacks and gain access to a wide range of other resources.

Social media accounts can become sources of risk even when they haven't been compromised. Users frequently post information on external social-media sites that attracts the attention of competitors or the media. To boost their job prospects, interns mention product features they helped develop during their summer job at a well-known company; sales representatives reveal the names of major clients; even senior executives have been known to unintentionally disclose key corporate strategies. In fact, services exist that specialize in aggregating apparently minor snippets of information from social-media and other web sites to build an accurate view of a company's size, geographical distribution, and business strategy, including hiring patterns that indicate whether the company is expanding and which new areas it is moving into.

Adjusting Behavior

To counter these new risks, we need to make employees aware and empowered, so they act as an effective part of the security perimeter.

At Intel, we have focused for several years on building security and privacy protection into the corporate culture, getting employees to own responsibility for protecting enterprise and personal information. Achieving this has required a lot of effort, and we've realized that it takes just as much work to maintain a culture of security and privacy as to build it.

Training is a key part of our efforts. We have found training is particularly effective when general security training, which fulfills most legal requirements, is supplemented by targeted training. Some roles and job duties pose a greater risk to data than others; employees who have access to sensitive information receive specialized courses that focus on their specific needs.

We've found that another effective technique is to embed security and privacy training into business processes. When an employee requests access to an application that handles sensitive information, they are automatically prompted to take training that focuses on the related security and privacy concerns. We have also moved toward online training, including video and other visually stimulating material as well as entertaining, interactive tools to help engage users. In the "Find the Phish" game, for example, users learn how to spot fake web sites designed to lure them into revealing personal information (see Figure 5-1).

Find the Phish: See if you can tell why these 5 Web sites are scams. Not sure? Click on the "Phish Clue" button to reveal the answers.

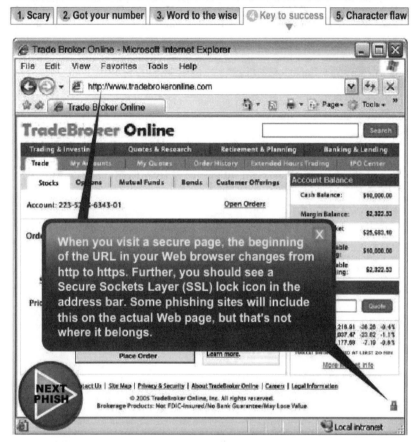

Figure 5-1. *Intel's internal "Find the Phish" interactive training tool helps employees spot web scams. Source: Intel Corporation, 2012*

However, it is not enough to create good training. If nobody takes the training, the effort is wasted. We have found incentives such as public recognition, combined with a training and awareness campaign, can help ensure employees undergo training and absorb the lessons. We promote training through positive messages, sometimes associated with themes such as online scavenger hunts. Ultimately, if people continue to avoid security training, we escalate compliance efforts by directly contacting them and their managers.

We've also found we can help maintain and increase awareness by publishing security-related articles on Intel's primary employee portal (see Figure 5-2 and the sidebar article). Many of these articles include a personal aspect, such as preventing identity theft, keeping children safe online, and home wireless security tips. We believe this personal aspect helps continuously reinforce our connection with employees and helps them more easily absorb the messages. The focus on personal concerns is also a recognition that the way employees behave outside the office is as important to enterprise security as their behavior in the office. These articles are also a good way to keep employees abreast of trends such as the growth of fake antivirus software. Other articles help to remind people of basic security issues, such as why it's important to avoid downloading applications from the Web, clicking mysterious attachments, and using weak passwords.

Figure 5-2. *Some of Intel's internal security-related articles for employees include a personal aspect, to encourage secure behavior both within and outside the workplace. Source: Intel Corporation, 2012*

HOW TO MAKE SURE NO ONE CAN ACCESS YOUR INTEL OR PERSONAL DATA ON YOUR SMARTPHONE

Ensure private information and Intel IP are properly protected with these simple steps

Story by: Secure Intel

Ahh, the good old days—when the only way to access your Intel e-mail account was through your laptop or desktop PC. But now, you can read corporate e-mail on your personal handheld device. Gone are the late call-ins to meetings because you had to wait for the bridge data-filled computer to boot up.

But with new conveniences come new necessary precautions. Because Intel e-mail is now available on our personal smartphones, it's important to take steps to protect the personal information and intellectual property we may be carrying on our handheld devices. How can you go about doing this? Easy:

1. Install a password on your iPhone (or other smartphone).

2. "Remote wipe" your smartphone if it's ever lost or stolen.

Just as we take steps to protect information on our laptops by installing encryption, we need to safeguard data on our smartphones. Password protection offers the first line of defense. But if you leave your phone in a restaurant or on a plane, a "remote wipe" can help increase the chances that your personal information—and Intel's intellectual property—doesn't fall into the wrong hands.

The Payoff

How do we know our security efforts pay off? We've accumulated a variety of evidence. These include independent benchmark results from the Information Risk Executive Council (2011), which indicate that over the last five years, Intel employees consistently ranked in the top 10 percent of companies for secure behavior.

We also experience laptop loss rates that are substantially lower than industry averages. Among more than 300 companies studied by the Ponemon Institute, the average rate of lost and stolen laptops ranged from 5 to 10 percent over a laptop's three-year lifespan. For the past several years, Intel's laptop loss rates have consistently been much lower than this, below 1 percent annually. I attribute this largely to our employees' level of commitment and sense of responsibility, in addition to the fact that we allow reasonable personal use of the laptop, as I'll discuss later.

We continue to observe examples of employees acting as part of the security perimeter. Recently, dozens of users alerted us to a suspicious text message they'd received via their personal or corporate smartphones. They thought the message looked odd and was potentially fraudulent. At the time, we didn't know whether this message was an exploit specifically targeting Intel, or a more widespread scam aimed at taking advantage of consumers in general. In a sense, it didn't really matter because a compromised personal environment can affect the security of the enterprise. By requiring employees to register their personal or corporate mobile devices, we have a database of all these devices. So we sent an alert to all of these users warning them of the problem.

This incident also illustrates how intruders are shifting to exploit new areas of vulnerability. As e-mail filtering improves, threats move to less-protected newer channels such as phone texting and instant messages.

In another less serious case, our human-resources group wanted to survey a broad cross section of Intel employees to gather their opinions of the company. They hired an outside agency, which dutifully e-mailed the survey to thousands of employees. Within minutes, our help desk phones lit up, as employees called to say they were receiving suspicious e-mails from outside the company. Administrative coordinators warned teams not to open the messages, and my security group began blocking the e-mails. Soon after this, we received an anguished call from the frantic manager who had funded the survey. Though this was frustrating for HR, it helped validate our security awareness work. After we had invested significantly in awareness campaigns, the employees' responses provided supporting evidence that we really had influenced behavior.

Roundabouts and Stop Signs

To try to reduce driving accidents at a dangerous curve in Chicago, the city painted a series of white lines across the road. As drivers approached the sharpest point of the curve, the spacing between the lines progressively decreased, giving the drivers the illusion they were speeding up, and nudging them to tap their brakes. The result was a 36 percent drop in crashes, as described by Richard Thaler and Cass Sunstein in their book *Nudge* (Yale University Press, 2008).

This traffic-control method succeeded in making drivers more aware and improving safety while keeping the traffic flowing with minimum disruption. I think this example provides a useful metaphor for information security. Some security controls are like stop signs or barriers: we simply block access to technology or data. But if we can shape the behavior of employees rather than blocking them altogether, we'll allow employees, and therefore the company, to move faster.

To use another traffic metaphor, a roundabout at an intersection typically results in more efficient traffic flow than an intersection with stop signs, because drivers don't have to come to a complete halt. The roundabout increases drivers' awareness, but they can proceed without stopping if the way is clear. Statistics have shown roundabouts are often safer than intersections.

Of course, we need to block access in some situations, such as with illegal web sites. But there are cases where it's more efficient and productive to make users aware of the risks, yet leave them empowered to make the decisions themselves. For example, it might make sense to warn users visiting certain countries that they may be accessing material that is considered unacceptable. Here's a hypothetical example. A US employee traveling on business might be working in a local office of a country with strict religious guidelines. The employee has a daughter who's in a beauty pageant—so it would be natural to check the pageant web site from time to time. But the images could be offensive in the country, so it makes sense to warn the employee to exercise caution. At Intel, we've found that when we warn users in this way about potentially hazardous sites, the vast majority heed the warnings and don't access the web sites.

In the case of information security, there's an additional benefit of making controls as streamlined as possible. We all know if controls are too cumbersome or unreasonable, users may simply find ways around them.

We kept this concern in mind when developing a social media strategy at Intel IT (Buczek and Harkins 2009). We were well aware of the risks associated with social media, but attempting to stop the use of external social media web sites would have been counterproductive and, in any case, impossible. We realized that if we did not embrace social media and define ways to use it, we would lose the opportunity to shape employee behavior.

As part of our initial investigation into this area, we conducted a social media risk assessment. We found social media does not create new risks, but can increase existing ones. For example, there's always been a risk that information can be sent to inappropriate people outside the organization. However, posting the same information on a blog or forum increases the risk by immediately exposing the information to a much wider audience. We also determined that we could reduce risk by implementing social media tools within the organization.

So we developed a social media strategy that included several key elements. We deployed internal social media capabilities, such as wikis, forums, and blogs. Initially, these were mostly standalone tools, and employees used them mainly to connect socially rather than for core business functions. Since then, our use has evolved to include more enterprise-focused tools, and we have integrated the tools into line-of-business applications to achieve project and business goals. We've also added social media tools tailored for specific business groups, such as a secure collaboration solution used by design teams to simplify real-time sharing of confidential project information across geographically dispersed teams.

As we designed our internal social media capabilities, we also worked with Intel's human-resources groups to develop guidelines for employee participation in external social media sites. Intel then developed an instructional video that was posted externally on a public video-sharing site. The video candidly explains Intel's goals and concerns, as well as providing guidance for employees. It explains that Intel wants to use social media to open communications channels with customers, partners, and influencers and to encourage people to adopt the technology, as well as close the feedback loop. The information also includes guidance about how to create successful content and general usage guidelines such as the need to be transparent, respect confidentiality, distinguish between opinion and fact, and to admit mistakes.

We also use technology to help ensure that employees follow the guidelines. We monitor the Internet for posts containing information that could expose us to risks, and we also monitor internal social media sites to detect exposure of sensitive information and violations of workplace ethics or privacy.

The Security Benefits of Personal Use

When it comes to technology consumerization, information security specialists tend to focus on the security risks. As I discussed earlier in the book, we've found that the productivity benefits easily outweigh the risks. But even the security implications are not as one-sided as they might seem at first glance. I believe that, in some respects, allowing personal use may actually encourage better security.

In general, people are likely to take better care of their own possessions than someone else's. They feel a stronger connection to their own car than to one provided by their employer. If people are using their own computing device, they may take better precautions against theft or loss. And they may feel the same way if they are storing personal information on a corporate device. At Intel, we allow reasonable personal use of corporate laptops, and therefore many employees store personal as well as corporate information on their laptops. Because of this, they have a personal stake in ensuring the devices don't get lost or stolen.

I believe this sense of ownership contributes to our lower-than-average laptop loss rates. And recently, another company's experience provided some empirical evidence supporting this idea. The company conducted a computing tablet pilot deployment in which, for the first time, it allowed personal use of corporate devices. At the end of the pilot, the company found that breakage and loss rates were dramatically reduced compared to its past experience with mobile devices. The CIO's conclusion was that employees simply take better care of devices when they use them for personal purposes. Due to the lower loss rates, the company saved money.

It may also be worthwhile to reexamine other assumptions about the security implications of personal devices. Some companies have policies forbidding the use of cameras in their offices. However, a smartphone includes a camera that employees can use to capture the off-the-cuff design sketches often scrawled on whiteboards during brainstorming sessions. This intellectual property can then be stored on a hard drive within the enterprise and encrypted. Is it safer to allow employees to photograph the image, or to copy it onto a piece of paper, or to leave it on the whiteboard where anyone might see it? Companies may come to different conclusions, depending on their culture and appetite for risk. But this is another illustration of the importance of considering all the possible business benefits, as well as the risks when making technology decisions.

Sealing the Gaps

Many organizations, including Intel, use disk encryption on laptops to protect data in the event the laptop is lost or stolen. Adoption of disk encryption accelerated when states began passing privacy protection laws, and the consequences of data theft increased as a consequence. However, with some disk encryption software, the latest data isn't encrypted until the user shuts down the PC or puts it into hibernate mode. If users simply put the PC into standby by closing the lid, the system may contain recently created data that is still unencrypted and vulnerable. If the PC is stolen at that point, the thief still has to penetrate the usual login access controls, but that's much easier than figuring out how to decrypt the data.

I realized many IT professionals were unaware of this when I spoke at a CIO conference soon after the first major privacy legislation was passed. I asked the audience how many of them had deployed disk encryption. Most raised their hands. I asked how many had experienced lost or stolen laptops since deploying encryption. Again, nearly all raised their hands. Then I asked how many of them had established a process for evaluating the state of a lost system to determine if the data on it was truly encrypted. This time, nearly all the hands stayed down.

I then explained why some laptops might contain unencrypted data, and asked how many of the audience thought they should issue a breach notification. At this point there was a silence, followed by a buzz of activity as attendees rushed off to make calls to security specialists at their companies.

When our security group analyzed this data encryption issue, we decided that we needed to be careful about how we addressed it. We wanted to ensure data on laptops was protected, but we didn't want to disrupt the users' experience by forcing them to shut down their laptops more frequently, and then endure the subsequent lengthy reboots. So we adjusted the system settings to initiate encryption whenever the laptop was left unused for a specific length of time. Now, if a laptop is lost or stolen, based on the time that elapsed since the employee last used it, we can determine the likelihood that it contains unencrypted data. While making this change to technical security controls, we also increased our efforts to educate employees about secure behavior.

The IT Professional

So far, in discussing the people perimeter, I've focused mainly on the security roles of end users. But let's not forget that IT professionals are also a part of the people perimeter, and that their actions can have major positive or negative effects.

IT professionals manage almost every element of the technology spanning our networks, data centers, and users' computing devices. They develop and install software. They configure, administer, and monitor systems. Their actions or inaction can make the difference between a system that is vulnerable and one that is reasonably secure.

Servers, which are typically managed by IT professionals, are still the IT assets most commonly attacked and robbed of data. An attacker may initially gain access to your company by compromising a user's laptop, but the biggest prize—databases of corporate intellectual property and personal information—still reside on the enterprise servers. To steal that information, the attacker may use a compromised end-user device to search the network for servers with inadequately configured access controls. Surveys show most attacks continue to exploit security holes that organizations could easily have fixed. Among organizations surveyed for the 2011 *Data Breach Investigations Report*, an astonishing 96 percent of breaches could have been avoided using simple or intermediate controls, and 92 percent of attacks were not categorized as highly difficult (Verizon 2011). "Every year that we study threat actions leading to data breaches, the story is the same; most victims aren't overpowered by unknowable and unstoppable attacks. For the most part, we know them [the attacks] well enough and we also know how to stop them," the authors concluded.

Similar trends can be seen in the incidence of software errors. Many of the most serious, frequently exploited vulnerabilities in software are due to well-known errors that are "often easy to find, and easy to exploit," as noted in the 2011 CWE/SANS Top 25 Most Dangerous Software Errors (CWE/SANS 2011). Furthermore, the situation does not seem to be improving. As David Rice, author of *Geekonomics* (Addison-Wesley Professional, 2007), puts it, most software is not sufficiently engineered to fulfill its designated role as the foundation for our products, services, and infrastructure (Rice 2007). This is partly due to the fact that incentives to improve quality are "missing, ineffectual, or even distorted," he concluded. To compete, suppliers focus on bringing products to market faster and adding new features, rather than on improving quality. Rice estimated, based on government data, that "bad" error-ridden software cost the United States a staggering USD 180 billion even back in 2007.

Not surprisingly, the typical recommendations for improving IT security often sound remarkably familiar. That's because they address problems already known to most organizations, but not fully addressed. For example, the recommendations of the *Data Breach Investigations Report* include ensuring passwords are unique; regularly reviewing user accounts to ensure they are valid and properly configured; securing remote access; increasing employee awareness using methods such as training; and application testing and code review to prevent exploits such as SQL injection attacks and cross-site scripting, which take advantage of common software errors.

The fact that these measures do not appear to be rigorously applied at many organizations takes us back to a key theme of this chapter: that the commitment of employees is as important as the policies and procedures you have in place. If IT administrators and enterprise developers are committed rather than just following directives, if they feel personally responsible for the security of the enterprise, they will be more conscientious about ensuring the right technical controls are in place.

Insider Threats

It's an unfortunate reality that many intentional threats originate within the organization. Among the 600 organizations participating in the 2011 Cybersecurity Watch Survey (CSO et al. 2011), about 20 percent of attacks were attributed to insiders.

The damage can be substantial. One employee working for a manufacturer stole blueprints containing trade secrets worth USD 100 million, and sold them to a Taiwanese competitor in hopes of obtaining a new job with them. Insider attacks also cause additional harm that can be hard to quantify and recoup, such as damage to an organization's reputation. Insiders have a significant advantage because they can bypass physical and technical security measures such as firewalls and intrusion detection systems that were designed to prevent unauthorized access.

Yet surveys have also suggested that many insider attacks are opportunistic, rather than highly planned affairs. Many insiders take data after they've already accepted a job offer from a competitor or another company, and steal data to which they already have authorized access. In some cases, misguided employees may simply feel they're entitled to take information related to their job.

It may not be possible to thwart all insider exploits, but we can take action to deter the more opportunistic attacks. Perhaps the biggest step we can take is to try to instill a culture of commitment. But we can also use technology to help against insider attacks.

As part of our security strategy at Intel, we're implementing monitoring technology that tracks users' logins and access attempts. At many companies, IT organizations treat such login data as information that should be closely held and not revealed to users. However, our strategy is to make login information available to users so that they can act as part of the perimeter, helping to spot anomalous access attempts. Let's say an employee's log indicates that he accessed the network from Asia yesterday, when in fact he was in Europe. The security organization might be unaware that anything untoward has occurred. But it's obvious to the employee that someone stole his smartphone or his access information, and he can alert us to the breach.

Providing this login information to users can also help deter insider attacks. If unscrupulous insiders know they're being watched, they're less likely to take advantage. It's like the corner store that invested in a CCTV camera; when you walk up to the counter, you see yourself in the display. Now consider the store on the next corner that lacks a camera. Which one is more likely to be robbed?

Finding the Balance

Whether we like it or not, people are already part of the perimeter. Technical controls alone are no longer able to keep pace with rapidly changing attacks, especially when those attacks are combined with sophisticated social engineering. It's up to us, as security professionals, to recognize that people, policy, and technology are all fundamental components of any security system, and to create strategies that balance these components. Above all, we need to create a sense of personal commitment and security ownership among our employees. If we succeed in this goal, we will empower employees to help protect the enterprise by making better security decisions both within and outside the workplace.

CHAPTER 6

■ ■ ■

Emerging Threats and Vulnerabilities

Reality and Rhetoric

Curiosity is lying in wait for every secret.

—Ralph Waldo Emerson

One day, it's hard to read an online news source, pick up a newspaper, or watch TV without seeing reports of new threats: cybercrimes, data breaches, industrial espionage, and potential destruction of national infrastructure. These reports inevitably leave the impression that we are drowning in an inexorable tide of new and terrifying threats.

One has to question how much of this is rhetoric, and how much is reality. There are political and profit-driven motives for making threats seem bigger and more imminent than they really are. US government officials have warned that cyber attacks potentially can be "devastating, approaching weapons of mass destruction in their effects" (Levin 2010). Such warnings have been used to justify requests for increased national cybersecurity funding, as well as proposed restrictions on private networks. It's not surprising, therefore, that some experts have expressed skepticism about the real extent of the threat. In fact, academics at the George Mason University Mercatus Center have warned, "the United States may be witnessing a bout of threat inflation similar to that seen in the run-up to the Iraq War" (Brito and Watkins 2012).

On the other hand, common sense tells us new cyber threats really are emerging and growing. Malware production has matured into a sizable industry. More data is online and vulnerable to attack, and millions of new Internet-connected devices are inevitably introducing new risks.

Given the flood of often-conflicting information, how can we get an accurate picture of the threat landscape so that we can develop an appropriate security strategy? How do we determine which threats directly affect our organizations, and distinguish them from those that are irrelevant? How do we decide which threats require immediate defensive measures, as opposed to those that attract attention but don't yet present significant risks?

In this chapter, I'll describe methods for identifying the real threat and vulnerability trends among the rhetoric. I'll also discuss some key areas of threat activity that have been analyzed using these methods. My goal is to help information security groups stay ahead of the attackers and focus their limited resources on mitigating the most important threats.

Structured Methods for Identifying Threat Trends

To identify the real trends in emerging threats among the mass of news and speculation, we need to carefully examine the available information using a structured, analytical approach. Unfortunately, many security groups absorb information about emerging threats using methods that are unstructured and sometimes almost haphazard.

A typical process looks something like this. The security team relies on external sources, such as news feeds and alerts, as well as informal anecdotes, to gather information about emerging threats. Based on this information, the team holds brainstorming sessions to review the threat landscape. The output from these sessions is a list of "top risks." Security resources are then focused on mitigating the items on the list.

There are several problems with this approach. Information comes from a narrow, limited range of sources, resulting in a blinkered security perspective that tends to stifle creative thinking. Also, the information is usually fragmented, making it difficult for the team to identify trends and gaps in the data. These deficiencies continue through security planning and implementation. Because the team lacks a full view of the threat landscape, it's hard to determine which threats require immediate attention and how much of the limited security budget they deserve. As a result, risks are incorporated into plans on an ad hoc basis, and not all risks are adequately mitigated. Finally, security teams often don't have a structured process for communicating threat information to other people within their organizations. Because of this, people outside the security group remain unaware of emerging risks and don't know how to respond when they experience an attack.

At Intel, we realized the limitations of this approach several years ago and began trying to inject more rigor into our risk-sensing strategy. Over time, we've progressively developed a more structured risk-sensing process that helps us identify threats, prioritize them, plan our response, and deliver actionable information to other groups across the company. Through continued use, risk sensing has become a systemic process within Intel.

Our process for analyzing emerging threats includes several valuable techniques that may be unfamiliar to security groups at most other organizations. We use a product life cycle analogy to track threats as they mature from theoretical risks into full-blown exploits. We also use nontraditional analysis techniques, such as war games and threat agent profiles, to encourage creative thinking and identify threats we might otherwise miss. I'll discuss these methods in more detail later in this chapter.

The process is managed by a small core team, supplemented by a broad set of experts across Intel. This arrangement ensures continuity while enabling the team to mine a diverse variety of sources to get a more complete picture of immediate and future threats.

Security team members research a wide range of individual security topics in depth. Besides using typical sources, such as external feeds and analysis, they mine academic research and hacker discussion forums, and they network with other security professionals. Other team members scan the regulatory horizon to identify upcoming laws and regulations that may impact us. We also analyze internal investigations and other near-miss incident data. Team members communicate with each other frequently to identify areas of potential overlap.

We then hold regular meetings to analyze the threat landscape. Each security domain expert explains their findings to other members of Intel's security community. For each security topic, we review recent events and then look ahead to the future. Reflecting on what has happened helps us identify the key trends and the factors driving those trends, and it provides context that we use to analyze the current state. We then look ahead to predict the likely evolution of each threat based on the trends we've identified.

This structured evaluation uncovers emerging risks we wouldn't otherwise see. We also look back at our previous predictions to see which ones were accurate, and to analyze the reasons why threats may not have materialized in the way we expected.

We communicate our findings to stakeholders across Intel in regular reports and briefings, including a wide-ranging annual assessment of the threat landscape. This communication provides further opportunities to get feedback from across Intel's business, which we can use to refine our risk-sensing analysis.

The Product Life Cycle Model

We have found that a product life cycle model is a useful way to track and prioritize emerging threats as they evolve and begin to present real risks to the enterprise. Like all security groups, we have a limited budget, and we need to direct our resources to mitigate the highest-priority threats.

This model, shown in Figure 6-1, recognizes that many threats initially emerge as theoretical risks, but are on a path to exploitation, and we need to evaluate and monitor them.

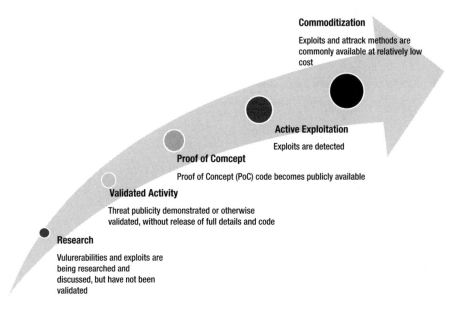

Figure 6-1. *The product life cycle model for tracking the evolution of threats. Source: Intel Corporation, 2012*

Often, researchers or hackers first reveal a possible attack or vulnerability at a security conference or publish information about it online. Next, attackers begin testing the use of this technique and making this information publicly available. Once the method has been proven, the threat enters the production phase as attackers start exploiting it in earnest. Ultimately, the threat becomes a mature commodity—source code is often freely available, many variants exist, and organizations treat the threat as part of the everyday landscape and build defenses accordingly.

This life cycle model enables us to systematically track the evolution of threats. It helps us determine when we need to allocate resources to fighting each threat. As each threat approaches maturity, we can examine how it is likely to affect us and plan appropriate mitigation.

In addition, at a product manufacturing company like Intel, this model provides a great way to communicate actionable information to business groups using terminology they understand—the product life cycle. When we provide our regular threat landscape assessments to stakeholders, each security topic includes a description of activity at each life cycle phase, thus providing a context that helps business groups across Intel determine how they should act on each of these emerging risks.

Let's examine some examples showing how we use this model in real life. Figure 6-2 illustrates the evolution of threats targeting smartphones and other handheld devices. Researchers and hackers began to take notice of handheld devices almost a decade ago, demonstrating weaknesses and theoretical avenues of exploitation. Initially, they focused on what were then known as personal digital assistants. As smartphones took off, attackers shifted their attention to this bigger market, which rapidly became a major area of threat activity. Monitoring this trend enabled us to prepare internally and inform Intel product development groups. As the threats matured and employees began using smartphones more widely at work, we then developed risk mitigation measures including technical controls and incident response plans.

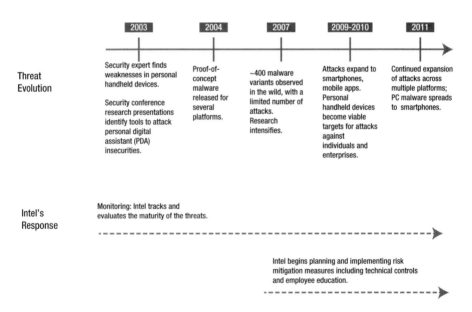

Figure 6-2. *How Intel used the product life cycle model to track and respond to smartphone security threats. Source: Intel Corporation, 2012*

By visually comparing activity across multiple threat areas, we can quickly identify major areas of activity and see the likely timing and extent of their impact. This chart shows the areas experiencing the most exploits today. It also shows us areas in which there are numerous proof-of-concept tests and other activities that suggest major problems in the near future. And it indicates areas of focused research that may ripen into active exploitation over the long term. Figure 6-3 shows how the activity in the areas of social computing and smartphones has shifted heavily to active exploitation, as previously predicted. It also shows an increase in research into threats to applications, which is likely to metamorphose into full-blown attacks in the future.

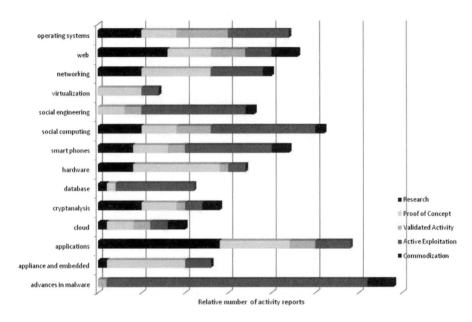

Figure 6-3. *A visual comparison of security-related activity across different technology areas. Data are for illustration purposes only. Source: Intel Corporation, 2012*

Though the depth of detail in Figure 6-3 is valuable to our security team, we have found a simpler, consolidated view can help communicate the essential trends to a broader audience. We have recently begun supplementing our threat analysis materials with charts like the one shown in Figure 6-4. These are based on the activity identified using the product life cycle model, but we add further trend analysis and group the activity areas into four main clusters, depending on their level of activity and maturity potential and on their potential impact to the company.

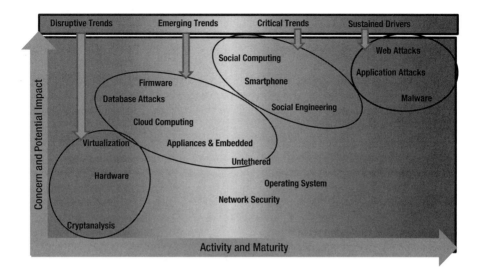

Figure 6-4. *Clustering areas of threat activity to highlight trends. Source: Intel Corporation, 2012*

These clusters are:

- *Sustained Drivers.* These are areas that already have a high impact or otherwise cause considerable concern. Typically, they are characterized by commoditized distribution and active exploitation by multiple threat agents. Today, examples include malware and web attacks.

- *Critical Trends.* These areas have begun undergoing active exploitation, with growing adoption beginning to shift toward commoditization. Current examples include social computing and smartphones.

- *Emerging Trends.* These areas have a low current level of exploitation, but considerable research and proof-of-concept activity. Examples include embedded and cloud computing.

- *Disruptive Trends.* These are areas with little or no active exploitation, but significant research activity and the disruptive potential to cause a major security problem. Frequently, they are discussed as theoretical risks, and because of this, many people in the industry would be caught off guard by a significant event. Examples include virtualization, an area in which potential threats and vulnerabilities have been exposed and a successful exploit could cause far-reaching damage.

We have found that clustering threat analysis information in this way enhances communication with stakeholders across Intel. Representing the information in easy-to-understand charts helps to convey the key trends and their potential impact to a broad cross-section of people, helping them quickly assess whether they need to make adjustments to security strategy.

Understanding Threat Agents

Besides the product life cycle analogy, we also apply other techniques that help us think creatively about threats and identify risks we might otherwise miss.

Behind every threat is a human agent. To effectively plan our defenses, it helps if we can understand why and how these agents operate: their motives, typical methods, and targets. However, we realized several years ago that we lacked agreed-upon definitions of threat agents, as well as a clear understanding of which agents actually pose the biggest risks to us.

Some agents and their activities attract considerable publicity, resulting in the "TV news effect:" the most-publicized agents appear to be the biggest threat, so they often receive a disproportionately large percentage of limited mitigation resources. In reality, a wide spectrum of threat agents exists, some of which may be less well-known but pose bigger threats. For example, hactivists often want to publicize their activities as much as possible to draw attention to their cause. This publicity makes them appear to be a bigger threat than other groups, such as organized crime syndicates, which try to conceal their exploits.

In addition, terms often are used without clear agreement about what they mean. The phrase *advanced persistent threat* has become a buzzword whose exact meaning depends on who is using the term. It usually implies adaptive, long-term strategies employing a variety of stealthy techniques and used by attackers with considerable resources. However, it's important to remember that a variety of agents may be capable of generating this type of threat. To understand and predict their likely motives and methods, it would be more useful to clearly define the agents, whether they represent nations or other powerful groups, such as organized crime.

To solve these problems, we developed a standard threat agent library that provides a consistent, up-to-date reference describing the human agents that pose threats to our information assets (Casey 2007). The library helps risk management professionals quickly identify relevant threat agents and understand the importance of the threats.

The library acts as a collection point for information about each agent, making it easier to share information across Intel. It includes profiles of agents such as disgruntled employees, opportunistic employees, industrial spies, and politically motivated attackers. The library also catalogs agents' typical targets, objectives, skill levels, current activity, and exploit outcomes. As part of our regular threat assessments, we determine which agents pose the biggest risks to Intel. We then can use the information about their typical methods and exploits to help plan our strategy. The library helps us understand why specific events and attack trends occur and what might happen next.

Playing War Games

We conduct war games a few times a year. War games are intense role-playing exercises in which Intel employees take on the role of attackers and attempt to compromise key assets using any feasible methods (Casey and Willis 2008). We have found war games are particularly valuable for analyzing threats that could have major consequences but whose vulnerabilities are not well understood.

This technique provides the most comprehensive method of assessing threats to key assets, because the people playing the role of our adversaries are essentially allowed to use any method to achieve their goals. However, because of this, it is also resource-intensive and should be used selectively.

A typical war game takes one and a half days and might involve eight to ten Intel staff from a variety of roles, such as factory workers, business process leads, salespeople, and technical experts.

The game focuses on a target or scenario, such as disabling a key facility or stealing Intel's trade secrets. We can use war games to examine potentially catastrophic events with a low probability of occurrence, but a high probability of causing damage if they do occur. The team members are instructed about the threat agents involved and draw on archetypes from Intel's threat agent library. Led by a facilitator, the team takes on the attacker's perspective and postulates ways to achieve the attack's objectives.

Because the team can propose any attack method, they often identify risks that might be overlooked using conventional methods. For example, a malicious group might attempt a devastating attack by purchasing a small but essential technology provider and inserting malware into their products in order to infect their customers. After each game, security analysts examine the results to determine how to address newly identified vulnerabilities.

At Intel, we also examine the cyber consequences of large physical events as part of our disaster recovery planning. These could include earthquakes and tsunamis that damage data centers, or even solar flares that disrupt the communications that the business relies on. Exercises can include drills that last a day or more.

A large company like Intel can justify the considerable effort involved in conducting these exercises because of the enormous potential benefit of mitigating the threats.

But smaller companies can also benefit by considering extreme events and formulating response plans. If you prepare for the extreme, you'll be more prepared to deal with everyday events. Planning doesn't need to be as resource-intensive as war games. It can be as basic as bringing team members together to discuss likely scenarios and responses. This method enables members to get a feel for what it would be like to work together should an actual disaster occur. Considering these extremes can also provide motivation for introducing simple yet effective measures to reduce the risk that catastrophes will occur. You might realize it is worth increasing investment in user education to reduce the risk of social engineering compromises, or becoming more diligent about analyzing logs and network traffic to identify patterns that indicate botnet activity.

Trends That Span the Threat Landscape

I've described some of the methods that can be used to analyze emerging threats. Now I'd like to turn to some of the key themes we have identified in emerging threat analysis conducted by Intel's information security group. These themes paint a broad-brush picture of threat and vulnerability trends spanning multiple technologies across the threat landscape.

Trust Is an Attack Surface

As the technology industry erects new technical defenses, attackers seek to bypass these controls by exploiting user trust—typically using social engineering techniques such as phishing.

If an attacker can win a user's trust with a sufficiently convincing e-mail or fake web site, the user will make it easy for the attacker by clicking a link or downloading a file. These actions usually undermine even the most rigorous system-level controls, initiating a chain of compromises that ultimately can result in major damage.

In 2011, this breach of trust was a common theme linking every major reported compromise. The initial stages of each of these compromises involved employees who trusted an external communication such as a targeted phishing attack.

Whenever users place their trust in a new technology, attackers quickly follow. Studies have shown users trust social media services more than other information sources—a user is more likely to click a link if it appears to have been sent by a social media "friend." Exploiting this trend, attackers have spread malware via social computing circles of trust such as friend networks.

Attackers have also been quick to take advantage of the trust users place in their smartphones and in other appliances, such as game consoles. The exploitation of trust also extends to the relationships between systems. Once configured, communications between systems often operate autonomously, without manual oversight. Smartphones are set to automatically update applications from trusted app stores; other systems blindly trust firmware updates and dutifully install them. This automation provides convenient opportunities to insert malicious code, abusing trust without the need to directly involve the user.

In the near future, we anticipate trust will become a commodity that is bought and sold. The digital reputation of systems and services will become critically important. In the past, tokens of trust, such as digital certificates and social computing credentials, were stolen for immediate use. In the future, they will be stolen so they can be sold in underground markets. The value of these tokens depends upon the access they grant and the other circles of trust they can be used to penetrate. Already, attackers are using stolen digital certificates to sign their malware in an attempt to avoid detection by operating system defenses.

I expect social engineering attacks will continue to present significant risks because they exploit human weaknesses and will adapt to take advantage of new technologies. So we, as security professionals, need to focus on the role of users as part of the security perimeter, as I discussed in Chapter 5. To reduce the risk to the enterprise, we need to make users more security-aware and influence them to act in more secure ways.

Barriers to Entry Are Crumbling

Our adversaries gravitate toward the path of least resistance. They tend to select targets that are easy to access and analyze, and they typically use the most readily available and cheapest tools.

They are much less likely to use methods with high barriers to entry such as the need for specialized expertise, expensive hardware or software, or access to extensive compute capacity. However, several of these barriers have begun to crumble as a result of trends such as cloud computing, lower-cost communications components, and commodity malware toolsets. This trend ultimately is likely to result in new types of attack.

A key factor is that security researchers are sharing not only their knowledge but also the tools they design as part of their research. Recently publicized tools, such as rogue base stations and Bluetooth sniffers, provide attackers with more accessible, low-cost ways to intercept network traffic. Researchers have uncovered vulnerabilities in *femtocell devices* (miniature, low-cost cell towers) that can be used to take control of the devices, lowering the barriers to attacks targeting cell phone data traffic.

Using a laptop and open-source software, a highly skilled researcher demonstrated the ability to create a base station to locate and communicate with a smartphone, then crash the mobile device and install rootkit or backdoor software on it.

Ultimately, lower barriers to entry mean increased risk to enterprises. However, because several of these areas are still at the research stage, it can take time for them to mature into active exploitation.

The Rise of Edge Case Insecurity

Each day, the environment becomes more complex with millions of new devices, each running its own operating system and collection of applications. This complexity generates new edge cases—problems or situations that occur only in unexpected or extreme situations.

Edge cases can include unlikely interactions between two familiar objects. A hacker team recently demonstrated that, with a popular smartphone, a paperclip (used to pop out the phone's SIM card at the critical moment), and a little patience, it's possible to gain access to contact information, phone call logs and voice mail, e-mails, and other information stored on the phone.

Overall, the growing number of third-party plug-ins and widgets introduce edge cases that are hard for developers to anticipate even if they use secure design techniques.

Interoperability between programs has resulted in a new category of hybrid attacks where malicious objects are concealed in innocent-looking ones to thwart detection. One proof of concept in 2011 demonstrated it was possible to conceal a fully functioning Trojan in an e-mail plug-in.

Some of these hybrid attacks have shown they can circumvent new security features. As web browsers and search engines try to protect users from malicious links, attackers are responding by hiding links in image search results, where they cannot be detected using standard tools. Research into network intrusion methods has discovered over a hundred methods of evading detection by manipulating traffic to remain functional but undetectable by typical tools.

There is no silver-bullet solution for eliminating edge-case insecurities. It's unlikely even the most rigorous testing could ever uncover them all. The best approach may be to exercise caution when adopting new technologies with the potential to generate edge cases.

The Enemy Knows the System

The technology industry has often relied on security through obscurity—the idea that if attackers can't see the insecurities in code or other technology, they won't exploit them.

Over time, it has become clear that security through obscurity is poor security. To quote the maxim coined by Claude Shannon, one of the founders of modern computing: "The enemy knows the system."

It's now relatively easy for attackers to get access to the same tools enterprises use, such as web hosting services and smartphone application development tools. Hackers can now more easily engineer malware and attacks that take advantage of these elements. The fact that static platform controls tend to become less effective over time (one of the Irrefutable Laws of Information Security noted in Chapter 1) is partly due to the ability of malware authors to pretest their malicious code against technical controls.

Even the success of social engineering demonstrates that the attackers' knowledge of the target greatly increases the likelihood of successful deception. Today, competitors and other threat agents learn a great deal about a company and its employees by simply searching information publicly available on web sites or social media accounts.

Because we cannot assume insecure technology is safe just because it is hidden, we need to design with security in mind. The ineffectiveness of security through obscurity is also an argument in favor of standards and open-source solutions. This idea may initially seem counterintuitive, but the fact that open source is exposed to public scrutiny requires it to be secure. At a minimum, we should ensure devices are rigorously tested against industry standards because the attackers will do so.

Key Threat Activity Areas

Threats are evolving in many technology areas, from embedded systems to cloud computing. I'd like to discuss a few areas experiencing significant developments with implications for enterprise IT.

The Industry of Malware

Malware has become a profitable industry that increasingly resembles the legitimate software market, with market leaders, mergers, licensing agreements, real-time support, and open source. The organized business activity in this market reflects the extent to which well-crafted malware has become a viable career pursuit for members of the criminal underground.

Today, malware development and malware use may be distinct activities carried out by different groups or individuals. Malware authors are producing standardized toolkits, which have made life much easier for would-be attackers. These attackers can now simply buy or acquire a toolkit rather than expending the effort to identify vulnerable web sites and develop their own exploits.

The Zeus malware family provides a useful case study showing how complex this industry has become and how hard it is to accurately track developments. Sold mainly in underground forums, Zeus has been used extensively for theft by creating botnet nodes. During 2011, a code merger was reported between Zeus and another popular crimeware kit, complete with assurances of future support for the customers of both products. Around the same time, Zeus toolkit source code was made publicly available. Since then, multiple new variants have appeared and been used for a variety of attacks. At one point, security researchers attempting to monitor Zeus exploits discovered a server they believed was the hub of a Zeus botnet. However, the server was the equivalent of an espionage honey pot, allowing the botmasters to turn the tables by spying on the researchers who were attempting to analyze the hub.

The Web As an Attack Surface

The Web continues to present a huge attack surface. And this attack surface is growing rapidly with the number of connected devices expected to expand to a billion or more. These include nontraditional devices such as appliances and control systems, cars, and the "smart" grid. Each of these is a potential source of risks.

For a glimpse of the probable future, consider the history of embedded devices in the enterprise environment. Companies have a history of deploying specialized devices without engineering security controls that reflect the risks these devices can introduce. Often, businesses deploy off-the-shelf devices without taking steps to harden them because of the perception that specialized devices are "dumb" and do not have a full set of capabilities.

In reality, the exact opposite is generally true. Devices marketed for a specific function are often capable of much more. Printers contain processors and may be capable of acting as file servers, for example. Furthermore, support for these devices is often outsourced, introducing a further source of potential risk in the form of external support technicians who enter the premises for monthly service visits. As a result, embedded devices can introduce as much risk, or more, to an organization as a traditional computing device since they lack security controls and administrators are generally unaware of the danger.

For attackers, embedded devices may become the path of least resistance. Embedded devices are always on and often poorly monitored. These devices store, transmit, and manage credentials and data, yet their default passwords are rarely changed. Some are initially configured to send data outside the network perimeter. Many can be remotely administered through web interfaces, making them viable points of attack. Furthermore, organizations often outsource on-site support of printers and other devices to an external supplier, who sends technicians to service the devices on a regular basis—introducing another potential source of risk that must be considered.

Security focus areas include printers and industrial control systems. In a recent example, researchers demonstrated they could replace printer firmware with fake updates capable of stealing information on documents sent to the printer, then forwarding this information to an external address. The vulnerabilities in industrial control systems were exposed by the widely publicized Stuxnet malware, which was used to sabotage systems with the apparent purpose of hampering Iran's uranium enrichment capabilities.

The incorporation of computer-based control and automation technology into the existing electrical power infrastructure—resulting in the "smart grid"—is another source of potential vulnerabilities. The US government has warned of increasing threats to the grid, noting that many embedded systems lack adequate security controls and are susceptible to known techniques such as cross-site scripting attacks (US GAO 2012).

Embedded devices, including medical equipment, safety systems, and locks, increasingly include wireless capabilities, so exploitation doesn't even require a physical network connection. Security researcher Jerome Radcliffe, a diabetic, remotely disabled his own insulin pump live on stage at the Black Hat conference in Las Vegas. Executing the attack required less than 60 seconds. In another celebrated example, researchers demonstrated a vulnerability in control systems at federal prisons that could allow an outsider to remotely take them over and perform functions that include opening cell doors.

We might also see logical attacks as precursors to physical attacks. On a macro scale, a nation state might attack another nation's cyber infrastructure before staging a physical attack. This approach might also be applied at a more personal level. A burglar might remotely disable an Internet-connected alarm system before sneaking into a house, or perhaps even use the system's video cameras to watch the owners and note when they leave the house unattended.

Smartphones

Smartphones are attracting almost as much malicious interest as desktop and laptop platforms. The adoption curve for smartphones is steep, with no end in sight. I expect the growth curve of smartphone malware to be at least as rapid.

Just as in legitimate software markets, malware authors are likely to maximize the value of their code by using tools that allow their software to run on multiple devices. They are increasingly targeting applications, a trend also seen on other platforms. A unique aspect of smartphone application attacks is the focus on application marketplaces, which present a convenient centralized location for disseminating malware. Attackers have purchased copies of applications, incorporated their malicious content into the otherwise legitimate software, and then redistributed their code under a new name or as a "free" version of the original. On one smartphone platform, autodialing malware was found in more than 20 applications. Variations of a Trojan were found in dozens of applications and are believed to have been downloaded by at least 30,000 users.

A further development is the use of smartphones as bridges to traditional networks, resulting in the potential for enterprise network attacks that originate from within mobile networks.

In the future, we could see greater exploitation of location-based services to deceive users. Because smartphones contain location sensors such as Global Positioning System (GPS) chips, knowledge of the phone's location can be used to present targeted ads and useful information. For example, a user in a supermarket aisle might be presented with online coupons for products on nearby shelves. But this information could also be exploited to present fake coupons that are all the more convincing because they suggest that the sender knows the user's preferences.

Attackers could also exploit other smartphone capabilities to take advantage of the fact that the devices are carried into confidential meetings and other highly sensitive situations. As security expert Dmitri Alperovitch recently observed (2012), "with remote control of a CEO's mobile phone, an advanced persistent adversary could activate the microphone to record private negotiations."

Current trends in the mobile platform space indicate attackers are most interested in stealing personal data. This trend is partly due to the increasing use of smartphones for financial and banking transactions, which provides new opportunities for identity thieves and other criminal groups. As a result, it is now important that smartphone hardware and software developers focus on protecting personal data. Software developers should adopt the same discipline and commitment to following secure design principles as traditional platform developers. Today, more and more people are becoming app developers—creating software and posting it online for others to use. One has to question how much security testing and validation has been applied to these applications. As users move more of their everyday activities onto smartphones and other small devices, the consequences of poor or insecure designs will have greater impact on individuals and their employers.

Web Applications

Web applications, primarily comprising client browsers and server-based applications, continue to be heavily attacked. In our threat analysis model, we characterize this area as experiencing full exploitation activity and moving toward commoditization. There is also considerable research in this area, suggesting the number of attacks will continue to grow.

Attackers have adopted new techniques to hide their intentions and deceive users long enough to achieve their aims. As web browsers and search engines try to protect systems from malicious links, attackers are instead obfuscating their links in image search results, where they may not be detected.

Techniques for hiding messages within images have been used within the security realm since long before the invention of information technology. Now, this technique, known as *steganography*, is being used to hide malware and botnets on publicly used image hosting sites.

Search poisoning has also become a common method. Attackers using search poisoning tend to focus on events and topics of popular interest, optimizing their web pages to achieve high search engine rankings. After a search query, the victim clicks a link among the search results. They are redirected multiple times and eventually land on a page that is used as a vector to deliver malware.

Conclusion

In this chapter, I've outlined some of the real threat trends and described methods information security groups can use to analyze the threat landscape as it continues to evolve.

No doubt, new and more-sophisticated types of exploitation will continue to emerge, and we need to stay aware of them. As Mustaque Ahamad, director of Georgia Tech Information Security Center, noted recently (2011), "We continue to witness cyber attacks of unprecedented sophistication and reach, demonstrating that malicious actors have the ability to compromise and control millions of computers that belong to governments, private enterprises, and ordinary citizens."

Yet, as we try to make sense of the deluge of news about attacks and vulnerabilities, it's essential to retain a sense of perspective. Most threats do not take place using exotic, obscure methods. Instead, they take the path of least resistance, exploiting well-known vulnerabilities. Therefore, business can mitigate many of these threats by implementing basic, established security measures. To put it another way: when you hear hoof beats, think horses—not zebras.

Social engineering will continue to be a key attack method because it takes advantage of user trust and is hard to prevent using technical controls. Therefore, as I discussed in Chapter 5, we need to continue to focus on educating users to become more security-aware. By doing so, we can reduce the risk to the enterprise.

Ultimately, while doing our best to prevent compromises and breaches, we must remember we cannot control the threat actors and their exploit attempts. For all organizations, some level of compromise is inevitable, making defense in depth as essential as ever. Losers ignore the trends. Winners survive by being able to predict, prevent, detect, and respond.

CHAPTER 7

■ ■ ■

A New Security Architecture to Improve Business Agility

Reality and Rhetoric

An organization's ability to learn, and translate that learning into action rapidly, is the ultimate competitive advantage.

—Jack Welch

Some *Star Trek* episodes feature suspense-filled battles in which adversaries use sophisticated phase-shifting weapons that can be rapidly adjusted until they find a way to penetrate static force-field defenses. For a beleaguered starship, the only effective response is to use similarly adaptable and fast-changing shields.

As information security professionals, we also need extremely agile defenses that can be quickly adapted to meet new demands. Attackers are continually adapting, and defenders also need to continually adapt. But rapidly evolving threats are only part of the challenge. The technology landscape is changing just as fast due to trends like IT consumerization.

As Intel's information risk and security group considers the future, we realize that we need to radically change our approach in order to face the challenges ahead and support the Protect to Enable mission. We need a more agile security architecture that can quickly learn and adapt to new challenges as they emerge. Because the environment is changing so quickly, in ways we cannot control, it's impossible to predict all the future challenges we'll need to face. We need an architecture that can learn to manage what we don't know.

This flexibility will help the business move more quickly, by enabling us to rapidly adopt new technologies and emerging usage models while continuing to provide security in the ever-evolving threat landscape. A learning system is harder to defeat because it can more quickly adapt in response to new attacks.

After intense brainstorming sessions, our information risk and security team devised a new security architecture. This architecture is our implementation of the Protect to Enable strategy.

In this chapter, I'll provide a high-level overview of the architecture and describe how it meets some key security challenges. Though the overview is based on our work at Intel, I believe that this is a novel approach to enterprise security that may be valuable to many other organizations facing these universal challenges. My conversations with peers at other companies have validated this view. Many of them are considering similar strategies and in some cases have begun implementing them.

We are implementing this architecture across Intel's IT environment in a radical five-year redesign of our information security technology. Even while the implementation is in progress, the new architecture has already delivered results by helping us provide innovative solutions to challenging use cases while actually reducing risk. Intel IT has published more detailed descriptions covering several aspects of the architecture (Ben-Shalom et al. 2011, Sunderland and Chandramouly 2011, Gutierrez et al. 2012), and we expect to continue to publish information in the future.

A key aspect of the architecture is that it provides more flexible, dynamic, and granular security controls than traditional enterprise security models. This helps us accommodate usage models such as bring-your-own-device (BYOD). We can provide users with different levels of access depending on factors such as the devices they are using and their location. To achieve this, the technology dynamically adjusts a user's access privileges as the level of risk changes. For example, an employee should have more limited access to our systems when using a less-secure device than when using a hardened, fully managed enterprise-class system.

The new architecture greatly improves threat management. As new risks appear, we need to be able to quickly recognize which ones we can mitigate, learn as much as we can, and take action as quickly as possible. At Intel, we use many information sources to gain an understanding of the risks. Collectively, these sources provide a continuous feed of collective intelligence that we can use to learn, adapt, and evolve. As I described in Chapter 6, we use emerging threat analysis to help us anticipate future risks. But our architecture also assumes that compromise is inevitable and focuses heavily on survivability. We are applying security monitoring and business intelligence to analyze patterns of behavior and detect anomalies that are symptoms of attacks. With this knowledge, we can further investigate and apply mitigation where necessary. In the future, this approach could be extended by automatically taking corrective action where it makes sense to do so.

Business Trends and Architecture Requirements

Before diving into the specifics of the architecture, I'll recap some of the key business and technology trends, focusing on how they drive the need for specific capabilities in security technology.

IT Consumerization

As I discussed in Chapter 5, consumerization is a major IT theme with ever-broadening impact. It includes several trends, including the adoption of new applications and support for consumer devices.

Many of Intel's highly mobile employees want to use their own consumer devices, such as smartphones and tablets, for work. This increases productivity by enabling employees to collaborate and access information from anywhere, at any time. To support this, we provide access to corporate e-mail and other applications from employee-owned smartphones and tablets.

Some people believe that in the future, all devices will be consumer-owned, and that enterprises will no longer purchase devices for their users. I believe this might be the case in some work environments, but I doubt that it will suit all organizations. For a company providing call center services, with most employees working from home, it might make sense that employees exclusively use their own personal systems for work. But this strategy would be more risky for a financial services company whose employees handle highly sensitive information that's subject to extensive regulatory requirements.

Nevertheless, the consumerization trend continues to grow at Intel and other organizations. Accordingly, we'll need to provide employees with a level of access to Intel resources from an expanding continuum of client devices, some of which have much weaker security controls than today's enterprise clients (see sidebar).

CONSUMERIZING ENTERPRISE IT AND "ENTERPRISING" THE CONSUMER

Discussions of IT consumerization tend to draw a clear line between business devices that can be managed and trusted, and personal consumer devices that are essentially unmanaged and untrusted.

However, not all consumer devices are created equal. From a security standpoint, it may be more valuable to think about a device's capabilities than to categorize it based solely on whether it's marketed as an enterprise device or a personal device. The security of a device depends on the inherent features of the hardware, operating system, and applications, and on whether it enables us to add further security and manageability capabilities that mitigate the risks of enterprise use.

As the variety of consumer devices, such as smartphones, continues to expand, users may choose from dozens of models with different levels of security capabilities. Greater security and manageability means that IT can place greater trust in the device and provide a correspondingly greater level of access to enterprise resources.

Extending this idea further, the information security group could evaluate the security of available consumer devices and provide guidance about the level of enterprise access that users will be allowed with each device. Users may prefer to buy a more secure device because it will provide them more access. With greater access, they can use the device for more of their daily work activities. This ability in turn enables them to be more productive.

At the same time, employees increasingly expect to have available to them at work the types of consumer services and cloud applications that they use in their personal lives. These include social computing applications such as blogs and wikis, video-sharing sites, and file-sharing services.

We need a security architecture that enables us to more quickly support new devices and provide access to a greater range of applications and data, without increasing risk. We need to be able to dynamically adjust the levels of access we provide and the monitoring we perform, depending on the security controls of the client device.

New Business Needs

Nearly all companies now rely on a growing network of business partners, and conduct many of their interactions with those partners online. Intel is no exception—we are developing an increasing number of systems for online collaboration with business partners. Also, like many companies, Intel is expanding into new markets through both organic growth and acquisitions. Because of these business trends, most organizations need to provide access to a broader range of users, many of whom are not employees. Many also need to be able to smoothly integrate acquired companies and provide them with access to resources. In general, we need to quickly provide new users access while minimizing risk and providing selective, controlled access only to the resources they need.

Cloud Computing

Most organizations are already using cloud services in some form to achieve benefits such as greater agility and lower cost. Like many companies, Intel IT is implementing a private cloud based on virtualized infrastructure, and we are also using external cloud services for noncritical applications. In the future, we expect greater use of hybrid clouds that use both internal and external resources.

This trend means that IT services at many organizations will be provided by a mixture of traditional and cloud-based internal and external services. During a typical day, employees may access a variety of different services, some of which are internal and some external. Ultimately, they should be able to easily move between these services without needing to log in multiple times or even know where the services are located.

Securing access to cloud-based services presents challenges that aren't easily addressed using conventional security controls. In cloud environments, systems and their data are virtualized and may migrate dynamically to different network locations. This makes it difficult to effectively restrict access using traditional security controls such as firewalls, which rely on fixed locations of systems and a more static nature of the data. We need much more granular and dynamic controls that are linked to the resources themselves rather than just their network location.

Changing Threat Landscape

The threat landscape is evolving rapidly. Increasingly, attackers are taking a stealthy approach, creating malware that quietly gains access and attempts to remain undetected in order to maintain access over time. As the number of threats increases and new types of malware emerge, we need to assume that compromise is inevitable.

Traditional enterprise security architectures have relied largely on preventative controls such as firewalls located at the network perimeter. However, our primary focus has shifted to providing controlled access to a broader range of users and devices, rather than simply preventing access. In addition, the continually changing threat landscape makes it necessary to assume that compromise will occur. Once attackers have gained access to the environment, the preventative controls they have bypassed are worthless. Although these perimeter controls will continue to have some value, we need tools that increase the ability to survive and recover once attackers have gained access to the environment.

Privacy and Regulatory Requirements

The growing emphasis on privacy requirements and the increasingly complex regulatory environment have many implications for the way we manage information. Some regulations create the need for more control over where information is stored and require specific levels of protection and tracking. Our architecture must provide this assurance, allowing us to build a high-security environment and access controls appropriate for the protection of highly regulated information.

New Architecture

To meet these rapidly changing requirements, we need a highly flexible and dynamic architecture. The architecture should enable us to more quickly adopt new devices, use models, and capabilities; provide security across an increasingly complex environment; and adapt to a changing threat landscape. At Intel, we formed a team chartered with designing this architecture from scratch, taking a fresh approach to enterprise security, then determining how to implement this new architecture across our existing IT environment.

Key goals include helping increase employee productivity while supporting new business requirements and technology trends, including IT consumerization, cloud computing, and access by a broader range of users. At the same time, the architecture is designed to reduce our attack surface and improve survivability—even as the threat landscape grows in complexity and maliciousness.

The architecture moves away from the traditional enterprise trust model, which is binary and static. With this traditional model, a user is in general either granted or denied access to all resources; once granted, the level of access remains constant. The new architecture replaces this with a dynamic, multitiered trust model that exercises more fine-grained control over identity and access control, including access to specific resources. This means that for an individual user, the level of access provided may vary dynamically over time, depending on a variety of factors—such as whether the user is accessing the network from a highly secure managed device or an untrusted unmanaged device.

The architecture's flexibility allows us to take advantage of trust that's built into devices at a hardware level, as well as trust in applications and services. Increasingly, devices will include hardware-enforced security designed to ensure the integrity of the applications and data on the device. The architecture takes this into account when determining whether to allow access to specific resources—a more-trusted platform can be allowed greater access than a less-trusted one. The architecture is based on four cornerstones:

- *Trust Calculation.* This unique element of the architecture handles user identity and access management, dynamically determining whether a user should be granted access to specific resources and, if so, what type of access should be granted. The calculation is based on factors such as the user's client device and location, the type of resources requested, and the security controls that are available.

- *Security Zones.* The infrastructure is divided into multiple security zones that provide different levels of protection. These range from trusted network zones containing critical data, with tightly controlled access, to untrusted zones containing less-valuable data and allowing broader access. Communication between zones is controlled and monitored; this helps ensure users can only access the resources for which they have been authorized and prevents compromises from spreading across multiple zones.

- *Balanced Controls.* To increase flexibility and the ability to recover from a successful attack, the model emphasizes the need for a balance of detective and corrective controls in addition to preventative controls such as firewalls. This includes a focus on business intelligence analytical tools to detect anomalous patterns that may indicate attempts to compromise the environment.

- *User and Data Perimeters.* Recognizing that protecting the enterprise network boundary is no longer adequate, we need to treat users and data as additional security perimeters and protect them accordingly. This means an increased focus on user awareness as well as data protection built into the information assets.

I'll describe each of the four cornerstones in more detail.

Trust Calculation

The trust calculation plays an essential role in providing the flexibility required to support a rapidly expanding number of devices and usage models. The calculation enables us to dynamically adjust users' levels of access, depending on factors such as the devices and networks they are currently using.

It calculates trust in the interaction between the person or device requesting access (source) and the information requested (destination). The calculation consists of a source score and a destination score, taking into account the controls available to mitigate risk. As shown in Figure 7-1, the result of this calculation determines whether the user is allowed access and the type of access provided.

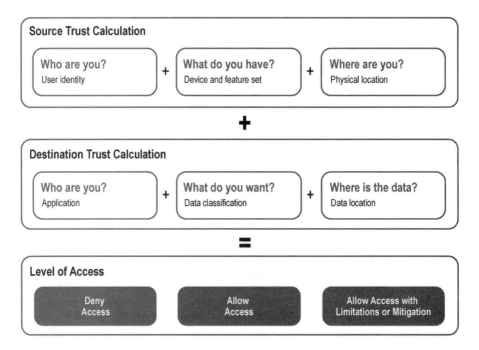

Figure 7-1. *Trust calculation. Source: Intel Corporation, 2012*

Source Score

Trust in the source, or requestor, is calculated based on the following factors:

- *Who*. The identity of the user or service requesting access and our confidence level in the authentication mechanism used—how confident are we that users are who they say they are?

- *What*. The device type, its control capabilities, our ability to validate those controls, and the extent to which Intel IT manages the device.

- *Where*. The user's or service's location. For example, a user who is inside the Intel enterprise network is more trusted than the same user connecting through a public network. There may also be other considerations, such as the geographical region where the user is located.

Destination Score

This is calculated based on the same three factors, but these are considered from the perspective of the destination—the information the source is trying to access:

- *Who*. The application that stores the requested data. Some applications can enforce greater controls, such as enterprise rights management (ERM), and therefore provide a higher level of trust.

- *What*. The sensitivity of the information being requested and other considerations, such as our ability to recover it if compromise occurs.

- *Where*. The security zone in which the data resides.

Available Controls

The trust calculation also takes into account the security controls available for the zone. If the only controls available are controls that simply block or allow access, we might deny access due to lack of other options. However, if we have extensive preventative controls with highly granular levels of access, detailed logs, and highly tuned security monitoring—as well as the ability to recover from or correct problems—then we can allow access without creating additional risk.

Calculating Trust

The trust calculation adds the source score and the destination score to arrive at an initial trust level. The available controls are then considered to make a final decision about whether access is allowed and, if so, how. This calculation is performed by a logical entity called a *policy decision point* (PDP), which is part of the authentication infrastructure and makes access control decisions based on a set of policies.

Based on the results of this calculation, the PDP makes a decision, allocating a trust level that determines whether the user can access the requested resource and the type of access that is allowed. Broadly, the decision will fall into one of the following categories:

- Allow access

- Deny access

- Allow access with limitations or mitigation

This trust calculation therefore allows us to dynamically apply granular control over access to specific resources. For example, employees using IT-managed devices with additional hardware features such as a trusted platform module (TPM), global positioning system (GPS), and full disk encryption would be allowed access to more resources than when using devices that lack those features.

Employees directly connected to the Intel network typically get greater access than when using a public network. If we are unable to verify the location of a high-security device such as a managed PC, we would allow less access.

The trust calculation also can be used for more fine-grained distinctions between different device models. For example, we could provide different levels of access based on smartphone manageability, hardware-enabled authentication and encryption, and installed applications.

We anticipate situations in which the trust level is not adequate to allow any access, but there is still a business requirement to allow a connection or transaction to occur. In these conditions, the result of the trust calculation could be a decision to allow access with limitations or with compensating controls that mitigate the risk. For example, a user might be allowed read-only access or might be permitted access only if additional monitoring controls are in place.

We're implementing this trust calculation across Intel's environment. Today, the trust calculation makes decisions based on information gathered from components at multiple levels of the infrastructure, such as network gateways, access points, and user devices. Once the trust calculation mechanism is in place, we can extend it to include information from a broader range of sources. For example, the calculation might take into account the level of hardware-enforced security features built into the user's device. This would allow us to provide greater access to users who have more-trusted devices.

The trust calculation can be used to determine access to internal systems by business partners as well as employees. Let's say we're collaborating with another company on the design of a new product. An engineer at that company wants access to a specific document. We can add a variety of criteria to the trust calculation for deciding whether to grant access. Did the engineer's request originate within the business partner's enterprise network? Is it consistent with the type of request that we'd expect from an engineer? If so, we have a higher level of trust in the requestor.

If we cannot establish an adequate level of trust in the user's device, but other factors provide enough confidence to grant access, we might provide one-time access for a specific job. We could do this by allowing a document to be downloaded, but only within a container that ensures the document is completely removed from the user's device once the job is completed.

Longer term, the trust calculation could become a mechanism that is used to determine access to both internal and external resources. Intel IT, like many companies, is using some external cloud-based applications, while developing an internal private cloud for most applications. In the future, we anticipate greater use of a hybrid-cloud approach. The trust calculation could be used to manage identity and access for both.

Security Zones

The architecture divides the IT environment into multiple security zones. These range from untrusted zones that provide access to less valuable data and less important systems to trusted zones containing critical data and resources.

Because the higher-trust zones contain more valuable assets, they are protected with a greater depth and range of controls, and we restrict access to fewer types of devices and applications, as shown in Figure 7-2. However, devices allowed access to higher-trust zones also have more power—they may be able to perform actions that are not allowed within lower-trust zones, such as creating or modifying enterprise data.

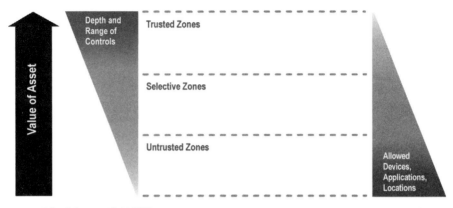

- - Policy Enforcement Point (PEP)

Figure 7-2. *As the value of an asset increases, the depth and span of controls increase, while the number of allowed devices, applications, and locations decrease. Source: Intel Corporation, 2012*

Aligning the infrastructure in this fashion provides an excellent way to right-size security controls so that security resources are utilized effectively. It also helps improve the user experience by enabling employees to choose from a wider range of devices, such as smartphones, for lower-risk activities.

Access to zones is determined by the results of the trust calculation and is controlled by *policy enforcement points* (PEPs). PEPs may include a range of controls, including firewalls, application proxies, intrusion detection and prevention systems, authentication systems, and logging systems.

Communication between zones is tightly restricted, monitored, and controlled. We separate zones by locating them on different physical or virtual LANs; PEPs control communication between zones. This means that if one zone is compromised, we can prevent the problem from spreading to other zones or increase our chances of detection if it does spread. In addition, we can use PEP controls, such as application proxies, to provide devices and applications in lower-trust zones with limited, controlled access to specific resources in higher-trust zones when required.

The architecture includes three primary categories of security zone: untrusted, selective, and trusted. Within the zones, there are multiple subzones.

Untrusted Zones

These zones host data and services (or the interfaces to them) that can be exposed to untrusted entities. This allows us to provide widespread access to a limited set of resources from non-managed consumer devices, without increasing the risk to higher-value resources located in other zones. Untrusted zones might provide access to enterprise resources, such as corporate e-mail and calendars, or they might simply provide Internet access.

These zones are regarded as "shark tanks," with a high risk of attack and compromise. Therefore, detective and corrective controls are needed to mitigate this risk. These controls might include a high level of monitoring to detect suspect activity and correction capabilities such as dynamic removal of user privilege.

We anticipate a need to provide controlled access from these zones to resources in higher-trust zones. For example, an employee using an untrusted device might be allowed limited, read-only access to customer data located in a trusted zone; or their device might need access to a directory server in a trusted zone to send e-mail. We expect to provide this controlled access using application proxies. These proxies act as secure intermediaries—evaluating the request from the device, gathering the information from the resource in a trusted zone, and passing it to the device.

Selective Zones

Selective zones provide more protection than untrusted zones. Examples of services in these zones include applications and data accessed by contractors, business partners, and employees, using client devices that are managed or otherwise provide a level of trust. Selective zones do not contain critical data or high-value Intel intellectual property. Several selective subzones provide access to different services or users.

Trusted Zones

Trusted zones host critical services, data, and infrastructure. They are highly secured and locked down. Examples of services within these zones are administrative access to data center servers and network infrastructure, factory networks and devices, enterprise resource planning (ERP) applications, and design engineering systems containing intellectual property. Accordingly, we might only allow direct access to these resources from trusted systems located within the enterprise network, and all access would be monitored closely to detect anomalous behavior.

At Intel, we have implemented secure high-trust zones as part of our transition to an enterprise private cloud. Implementing these zones was a key step in allowing us to move several categories of application onto virtualized cloud infrastructure, including internal applications requiring high security, as well as externally facing applications used to communicate with business partners. The security features in these trusted zones include application hardening and increased monitoring. We continue to add further security capabilities over time.

NEW SECURITY ARCHITECTURE IN ACTION: A DAY IN THE LIFE OF AN EMPLOYEE

This example (illustrated in Figure 7-3) describes how the new security architecture enables the Intel sales force to access the information they need in the course of a day. At the same time, the architecture protects Intel's security by dynamically adjusting the level of access provided, based on the user's device and location, and by monitoring for anomalous behavior.

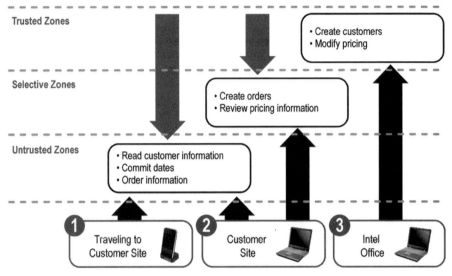

Figure 7-3. *The new security architecture dynamically adjusts the user's access to information, based on factors such as the user's device and location. Source: Intel Corporation, 2012*

The employee travels to a customer site. The employee is using a personal smartphone with limited security features and so is allowed access only to services in untrusted zones. From here, the employee can view limited customer information, including recent orders, extracted from an enterprise resource planning (ERP) system in a trusted zone—but only through an application proxy server, which protects the trusted zone by acting as an intermediary, evaluating information requests, accessing the ERP system, and relaying the information to the user.

If a smartphone requests an abnormally large number of customer records—an indication that it may have been stolen—further access from the smartphone is blocked. To help understand the reason for the anomalous access, there is increased monitoring of the employee's attempts to access the system from any device.

The employee reaches the customer site and logs into the enterprise network from a company-owned mobile business PC. Because this device is more trusted, the employee now has access to additional capabilities available in selective zones, such as the ability to view pricing and create orders that are relayed by an application proxy to the ERP system in a trusted zone.

The employee returns to the company's office and connects to the corporate network. Now the employee is using a trusted device from a trusted location and has direct access to the ERP system in a trusted zone.

Balanced Controls

Over the past decade, enterprise security has focused heavily on preventative controls such as firewalls and intrusion prevention systems. This approach offers clear benefits: it is less expensive to prevent an attack than to correct problems after one has occurred, and it is easy to see when firewalls have successfully prevented an attempted compromise.

However, the new security model requires that we balance preventative controls with detective (monitoring) and corrective controls, for several reasons.

First, the focus of the new model is on enabling and controlling access from a wider range of users and devices, rather than on preventing access. Second, the continually changing threat landscape makes it necessary to assume that compromise will occur; all preventative controls will eventually fail. Once attackers have gained access to the environment, the preventative controls they have bypassed are worthless.

By increasing the use of detective controls and implementing more aggressive corrective controls, we can mitigate the risk of allowing broader access. These controls also increase our ability to survive and recover from a successful attack.

USING SECURITY BUSINESS INTELLIGENCE TO DETECT SUSPICIOUS BEHAVIOR

Like any large organization, Intel has experienced security issues involving both external attackers and insiders, including attempts to steal intellectual property. As we've investigated, we have identified markers and indicators that are frequently associated with these events. We realized that if we had been able to spot these indicators sooner, we could have responded and mitigated the threats more quickly.

Security business intelligence is a key technology that we can use to detect suspicious behavior as the environment becomes more complex and attackers become more adept at concealing compromises. Analytical tools automate the process of analyzing large volumes of data to detect and monitor anomalous activity, allowing us to detect problems that we might otherwise miss.

These capabilities are similar to those already implemented by financial institutions to prevent fraudulent credit-card transactions, and by online consumer services to prevent theft of user data. Banks monitor access attempts and online transactions to determine whether to trust the user's identity and whether to allow the user's activity. If the user is trying to transfer a large sum to an external account, the bank's systems may compare the transaction with the user's previous behavior to see if it appears to be abnormal. To mitigate risk, the bank may delay large transfers so it can perform additional analysis and inform the account owner by e-mail.

In a similar way, we can use security business intelligence—analysis and correlation of data gathered by monitoring—to analyze patterns of behavior. This can detect and thwart possible attacks.

On a large scale, logging data generated by servers and sensors across the network can be collected into a database for analysis. At Intel, we are using analytic tools to correlate this aggregated data and flag anomalies for further investigation. For example, if traffic within a server cluster becomes abnormally high, it might indicate that a botnet is exploiting one of the servers to broadcast traffic across the Web.

Security business intelligence can also be applied at the level of individual users and devices. At Intel, we're implementing monitoring technology that tracks users' logins and access attempts, as I described in Chapter 5. Our strategy is to make login information available to users so that they can help to spot unauthorized access attempts.

In the future, I envisage that the system could analyze users' historical behavior patterns to determine how to respond when users request access to resources. The system could compare the request with the user's previous actions: what have you done before, and is this request consistent with those behaviors or is it an anomaly and therefore suspicious? If the request appears consistent with previous behavior, the system would pass the request to the trust calculation; if it appears anomalous, the system might deny the request and alert the security team.

Within Intel, we have also deployed a dashboard that provides granular information about infected clients and servers, boosting our ability to intervene quickly and accurately. Due to our efforts to detect and remove malware before infections occur, we achieved a 33 percent reduction in malware impacts in 2011, despite experiencing a 50 percent increase in the number of variants (Intel 2012a). We also plan to add a predictive engine that enables proactive protection and simulations that can improve our ability to respond to threats.

The balance between preventative, detective, and corrective controls will vary, depending on the security zone. In high-trust zones, we implement extensive monitoring to detect possible attempts to steal data or compromise critical systems. Redundancy within each type of control can be used to provide additional protection.

The following includes possible examples of using detective and preventative controls:

- An Intel employee attempts to send a confidential document to a non-Intel e-mail address. Monitoring software detects the attempt, prevents the document from being sent outside the firewall, and asks the Intel employee if he or she really intended to do this. If the employee confirms that this was intended, the document may be transmitted—or if the document is highly sensitive, a redacted version may be sent.

- Inappropriate use of a document protected with enterprise rights management technology results in revocation of access to the document.

- The system allows access to specific documents but tracks the activity. A user can download a few documents without causing concerns. However, if the user attempts to download hundreds of documents, the system slows down the speed of delivery (for instance, only allowing ten to be checked out at a time) and alerts the user's manager. If the manager approves, the user is given faster access.

- The detection of an infected system places the system on a remediation network, isolating the system and restricting access to enterprise information and applications. The system may retain some ability to access corporate assets, but all activity is closely logged to enable incident response if necessary.

- When a system is found to be compromised, we examine all its recent activities and interactions with other systems. Additional monitoring of those systems is automatically enabled.

Users and Data: The New Perimeters

The concept of balanced controls also extends to the protection of users and data. Traditional network security boundaries are dissolving with the proliferation of new devices and users' expectations that they should be able to access information from anywhere at any time. Users are under direct assault from a barrage of attacks designed to trick them into taking actions that can compromise the information on their devices or on enterprise systems. These trends mean that we need to think more broadly about how we protect information, as well as the users of this information.

While we continue to implement enterprise network controls, such as perimeter defenses and the detective controls described earlier, we need to supplement these controls with a focus on the users and on the primary assets we are trying to protect such as intellectual property. The new architecture therefore expands our defenses to two additional perimeters: the data itself and the users who have access to the data.

Data Perimeter

Important data should be protected at all times—when it is created, stored, and transmitted. This becomes increasingly challenging as we move data to more and more devices and let more people access it. How do we protect information when it's located outside the physical perimeter on a personal device?

At Intel IT, we're implementing technologies that closely integrate protection with high-value data so that the data remains protected as it moves to different devices and locations. Technologies, such as enterprise rights management and data leak prevention, can be used to watermark and tag information so that we can track and manage its use. With enterprise rights management, the creator of a document can define exactly who has access rights throughout the life of the document and can revoke access at any point. Data loss prevention is used to tag documents, track their movements, and prevent transfer outside the organization if necessary.

User Perimeter

As I described in Chapter 5, people are part of the security perimeter, and we need to treat them as such. Users can become security risks for a variety of reasons. They are targeted more frequently in social engineering attacks, and they are more vulnerable to these attacks because their personal information is often readily available on social networking sites. They may also click malicious links in e-mail, download malware, or store data on portable devices that then are lost.

At Intel, we've found that a combination of training, incentives, and other activities can help instill information security and privacy protection into the corporate culture and successfully encourages employees to own responsibility for protecting enterprise and personal information. We've seen our efforts pay off, with employees calling the help desk or sending e-mail alerts when they notice something that doesn't seem right. As discussed in the sidebar ("Using Security Business Intelligence to Detect Suspicious Behavior"), our strategy also includes making account access logs available to users so that they can help spot unauthorized access attempts.

Conclusion

This chapter describes a new architecture designed to support the Protect to Enable mission. Its goal is to allow faster adoption of new services and capabilities while improving survivability. At Intel, we believe that this architecture can be used to meet a broad range of evolving requirements, including new usage models and threats. Because of this, we are working to ingrain this model into all aspects of Intel IT, from development to operations. We've already used aspects of the architecture to provide solutions to challenging use cases, while actually reducing risk. For example, we've been able to move important internal and Internet-facing applications to a private cloud by utilizing high-trust zones. We've successfully used various approaches to protect the user and data perimeters. We also used balanced controls and trust zones to enable network access from employee-owned devices. In some cases, projects have seen their security overhead decrease by adopting this model.

I believe that the architecture could provide similar value to other organizations facing similar challenges. By publishing information about the architecture, we hope to encourage others to take advantage of this architecture wherever it meets their needs. We also hope that making this information available will stimulate more discussion and ideas, and that others will build on these concepts to create further innovations that benefit all of us.

CHAPTER 8

Looking to the Future

Emerging Security Capabilities

Learn from yesterday, live for today, hope for tomorrow. The important thing is not to stop questioning.

—Albert Einstein

The Web has existed for two decades, yet it's only in the last few years that we've gained a clearer picture of what the Internet may become, and how the emerging capabilities may shape the future.

As early as 1993, companies like AOL started offering access to online newsgroups, soon followed by dial-up Internet access using early web browsers. As laptops became more affordable, many people started accessing the Internet while on the move. The rise of smartphones introduced built-in sensors, such as cameras, global positioning system receivers, and touch-sensitive screens, into consumers' everyday computing experiences. Businesses began using the information gathered from users' devices to offer personalized experiences, ranging from location-based driving directions to selected advertisements. The variety of Internet-connected devices rapidly expanded to include tablets, home DVRs, appliances, and cars. Devices also became smarter, with improved voice and gesture recognition.

We're now entering a world in which these elements will be combined to create much richer context-aware experiences for users and new opportunities for businesses. Our devices will know us, and they will know other devices. In fact, devices may almost become part of us: many companies are working on wearable computers, including technology embedded in clothing to diagnose sleeping problems and self-adjusting prosthetics to enable amputees to walk more naturally. To improve our fitness, smart garments may monitor our bodies' performance and send the information to a handheld device, on which a virtual trainer app will create "tailored workouts that know you better than you know yourself" (Etherington 2012).

Each day, billions of computing devices will perform functions on our behalf, often communicating among themselves to get the job done. Much more information will be collected from sensors such as cameras, microphones, and GPS receivers embedded into the user devices. This data will be combined with other information to create context-aware experiences that are far more personalized and compelling. Already, cameras and image recognition technology, combined with behind-the-scenes analytical software, can be used to identify a user's age bracket and gender, and tailor their experience accordingly. Early applications based on this technology are being piloted and in some cases deployed by large companies, including retailers (see sidebar).

Context-aware technologies are expected to create huge business opportunities affecting an estimated USD 96 billion of annual consumer spending worldwide by 2015, according to Gartner, Inc. (2011a). By that time, more than 15 percent of all payment card transactions will be validated using contextual information, the research firm estimates.

RICHER EXPERIENCES IN THE RETAIL ENVIRONMENT

As they seek to entice customers into stores, retailers are experimenting with technology that provides a glimpse into how future shopping experiences could be richer and more context-aware. Several of these solutions, developed in collaboration with Intel, are entering the pilot stage or already deployed (Intel 2012).

LEGO brand retail stores give shoppers the opportunity to star in a game as a LEGO Minifigure, in which an animated character mimics the player's movements. Featured at a branded store in Chicago, the interactive window display uses animation and gesture recognition software.

Adidas created a virtual footwear wall that addresses a common problem—when shoppers visit a store, they often can't find the exact shoe model or size they need. The virtual footwear wall demonstrates how retailers can give in-store shoppers access to much more detailed information about their expanded online inventory via a digital display. The display detects the shopper's age bracket and gender, and displays an appropriate selection of shoes. Using touch screens, shoppers can select products from a virtual shelf, view them from any angle, zoom in for more detail and technical information, see what others are saying on social networks, and ultimately purchase products directly from the wall.

Several other retailers are using technology that detects a user's approximate age and then uses the information to offer personalized services. Among them is Kraft Foods, which created a product sampling platform that dishes up complimentary samples of Temptations desserts—offered to adults only, of course.

These new technologies also introduce new risks, as I described in the discussion of emerging threats and vulnerabilities in Chapter 6. The sensors and other new capabilities embedded into millions of intelligent new devices can be exploited for malicious purposes. Malicious individuals might be able to remotely access home security surveillance systems to determine when you're not at home. Attackers might try to remotely control the brakes and other functions of an Internet-enabled car.

As security professionals, we may tend to focus obsessively on this darker side of the picture. Looking for threats and vulnerabilities is part of our role. We've seen that attackers find ways to exploit new technologies almost as soon as they appear. Analysis of emerging threats conducted by Intel's information risk and security group indicates that this trend will continue. As attackers adapt, we must adapt, too. In fact, our role will be more important than ever. As more aspects of people's daily lives are based on technology, it will become increasingly important to secure the technology. The Protect to Enable mission will expand accordingly.

The positive news is that new technologies can also be used to enhance security. As information risk becomes an even more high-profile concern, suppliers are building more security into their products and services. Devices will include a greater level of baseline security hardening to reduce the likelihood of compromise and minimize the impact.

Context-aware computing also introduces new privacy concerns. By definition, context-awareness involves taking advantage of information about the user to create personalized experiences. This makes it even more important to appropriately protect users' information and privacy. A clear organizational commitment to privacy will be important to ensure this protection. Intel, like a growing number of other organizations, has formally committed to compliance with a single set of privacy rules worldwide.

An organization's privacy commitment must also extend to applications and systems. Suppliers are becoming increasingly aware of this, and some are already taking additional steps to ensure user data is collected anonymously. The new baseline security capabilities built into products, such as hardware-enforced protection and accelerated encryption, may also help enhance privacy by protecting user data. In addition, the information provided by sensors can be used to create context-aware security. Today, some cars can automatically adjust seat, mirror, and pedal positions to suit different drivers. They adjust these settings when they detect the presence of the driver's personal car key. In the future, as cars become more intelligent and include more sensors, they might identify the driver using a camera and microphone. If they don't recognize the driver, they might disable the car and alert the owner via their built-in wireless Internet connection. Cars might include a maintenance mode that lets mechanics drive it while when it's being serviced, but only within a radius of a few miles. Similarly, as I'll discuss later in this chapter, the sensors in an enterprise-class device, such as a business laptop PC, could be used to prevent theft and help protect the information it contains.

From the perspective of the enterprise information security team, these emerging capabilities will allow increased trust in users and their devices. When we have a higher level of trust, we can provide the user with greater access to sensitive enterprise information and other resources.

The idea of dynamically evaluating trust is a key aspect of the new security architecture that we're implementing at Intel IT, as I discussed in Chapter 7. Employees may want to access our systems from a variety of devices and locations—including personal smartphones and tablets as well as business PCs. When a user requests access to enterprise systems, our architecture will dynamically calculate trust based on contextual information such as the user's identity, the security features of the device they're using, their physical location, and the resources they're trying to access. The architecture then will decide whether to grant access, and the level of access that should be allowed. As manufacturers increase the security capabilities in their devices, our model will be able to take this into account. We'll have increased trust in a device, and we'll be able to provide a correspondingly greater level of access.

In this chapter, I'll take a closer look at some of the emerging security capabilities that we can expect in products and services. First, though, I'd like to set the stage by examining some of the key underlying trends that make these security capabilities both necessary and possible.

Internet of Things

Many everyday objects are becoming more intelligent. They're acquiring processors, sensors, software, and the ability to communicate. This trend is made possible by Moore's law: processors and other hardware components continually become faster and less expensive, and, therefore, ubiquitous as a result. This accelerating trend is creating the Internet of Things—a massive expansion of the Internet as it swells to include billions of devices and household objects. Intelligent devices in cars, home electronics, and other "things" may far outnumber those in more conventional computing platforms and even those in mobile devices such as smartphones. Intel estimates that by 2015, more than 15 billion connected devices will be in use (Intel 2011).

Gartner, Inc. (2011b) identifies several key technologies and capabilities contributing to this trend, including sensors, image recognition, and wireless payments using *near field communications* (NFC) technology. Sensors that detect and communicate changes in their environment are being embedded not just in mobile devices, but in an increasing number of places and objects. Emerging applications will take advantage of this information. For example, camera-based image recognition technologies are expanding from mainly industrial applications to broad consumer and enterprise uses. These systems gather information about users and then analyze this information to personalize the user experience. Intel is working with a number of retail companies to build experiences that include image recognition (see sidebar). Wireless NFC, based on an emerging communications standard analogous to the Radio Frequency Identification (RFID) technology already established in some industries, lets users make payments by waving a mobile phone in front of a compatible reader.

With technologies such as NFC, the concept of the Internet may broaden to include an even wider variety of "dumb" objects, like drink cans or fertilizer bags (Gartner 2011b). This trend will provide opportunities for innovations that were not previously possible. Today, items in stores may include 2D bar codes that can be read by smartphones. In the future, store items may include NFC on the packaging or shelf label allowing them to wirelessly identify themselves to nearby devices, such as a shopper's smartphone. The shopper will then be able to learn not only about the product, but also alternatives, and could even view cross-selling and up-selling suggestions.

Devices such as the Nest Learning Thermostat may provide a glimpse of the future. This home heating controller is designed to be intuitive and simple to operate, replacing complex menus and instructions with a single big button and a dial (Nest Labs 2012). Users can remotely monitor and set the temperature from their smartphones, so they know the house will be warm by the time they get home. But perhaps the most interesting capability is that, as its name suggests, it can learn. The Nest monitors use of the heating system and attempts to learn the user's preferences—when the heating is switched on and off, and the desired temperature. After studying the use patterns for a while, the Nest begins to predict and autonomously set the temperature and timing itself.

I believe that devices like this are early examples of a much larger trend. As the Internet of Things grows, more interactions will occur directly between devices, rather than between people and device. Devices and objects will interpret and act on information provided by other objects. This will enable much more intuitive and streamlined experiences in many different fields. Consider the following scenario, described by Plantronics CTO Joe Burton (2012). A doctor visits a patient in a hospital room. A smart device the doctor is wearing turns on the doctor's workstation in the room, then authenticates the doctor to the patient management system, detects which patient is near the doctor, and pulls up the patient's record. When the doctor leaves the room, the information accumulated during the visit is saved and the workstation powers down.

Compute Continuum

Users now demand the same quality of experience in the workplace that they've become accustomed to in their personal lives. This includes the ability to access information across a continuum of devices, including PCs, smartphones, and tablets. They expect to be able to move from one device to another. They also expect intuitive applications on all of these devices, with the application's features tailored to the device's size and capabilities.

IT therefore needs to provide users with a consistent experience across devices and the ability to seamlessly transition between them. As enterprise information security professionals, we need to focus on the user experience and on enabling this broader range of devices while managing the risks.

Cloud Computing

The cloud is as much a new business model as it is a technology shift. The ability to obtain flexible IT services on demand lets businesses operate more dynamically—quickly taking advantage of business opportunities and growing or shrinking infrastructure capacity to meet demand. Cloud services can also potentially reduce cost.

However, cloud computing can also add new security complexities and data-protection concerns. Organizations may use multiple cloud providers, while also operating a private cloud for the most sensitive applications. Users need to be able to easily access services delivered from any of these multiple environments. From the enterprise perspective, we need to enable a seamless user experience while minimizing risk. This implies a federated model in which the user needs to log in only once; the user's credentials can then be used to access multiple applications. However, this also means that an attacker may only need to gain access once in order to compromise several environments.

Business Intelligence and Big Data

Businesses have quickly realized the value of analytical tools for real-time analysis of massive amounts of unstructured data. In the future, these analytic capabilities will increasingly be used to interpret data from sensors as well as from databases, social media, and other sources. The analysis of this information will then be used to create new personalized experiences, like the retail examples discussed in the sidebar "Richer Experiences in the Retail Environment."

This analysis can also be integrated with existing enterprise systems to create sophisticated customer-focused services. Here's a scenario described by Accenture (2012): a rental car company automatically detects when an accident with one of its cars has happened, initiates emergency services if needed, and issues a replacement rental car to meet the renter at the scene, greatly improving the chances of creating a loyal customer for life.

Business Benefits and Risks

By now, it should be apparent that the richer experiences enabled by these capabilities are as important to businesses as they are to users. New, context-aware experiences may attract customers and create new revenue. Furthermore, focusing on the user experience may be essential for business survival. If we don't provide rich and appealing user experiences, customers may gravitate toward competitors that do.

Our challenge is to manage the risks associated with these new experiences. The good news is that new security capabilities are emerging to help us do so.

New Security Capabilities

The IT ecosystem is increasingly focusing on building security into hardware, software, and services. We'll all be able to take advantage of this security to protect users and the enterprise. I think of these capabilities as the equivalent of termite-resistant building materials used in construction. They may not prevent termite attacks altogether, but they can stop some of them and minimize the impact of others.

Suppliers will need to frequently enhance these defenses to ensure they remain effective. As I noted in Irrefutable Law #6 in Chapter 1, security controls operate in a dynamic environment in which attackers are constantly learning and adapting their approach. Unless the defenses also adapt, they will lose their effectiveness over time.

I expect the ecosystem will increasingly view these security features as a way to differentiate products to meet the needs of distinct categories of customers. As a parallel, think about how the auto and other consumer industries developed. Initially, manufacturers focused on getting the public to buy cars en masse. Accordingly, the focus was on mass-producing just a few models at the lowest cost. As Henry Ford famously said, "Any customer can have a car painted any color that he wants so long as it is black" (Ford and Crowther 1922). Ford's mass-production strategy was enormously successful in popularizing cars among the American public. By 1918, half of all cars in the United States were Model Ts (The Henry Ford Museum 2003). But once consumers became more familiar with cars, they started demanding models that met specific needs. As manufacturers responded, the industry began to develop the huge variety of models that we see today.

In the same way, suppliers will offer a range of products or services with differing levels of security, including higher-security versions for the most sensitive enterprise uses and less-secure versions for consumers. This trend has already been evident for some time in products such as servers and PCs, and we're beginning to see it in cloud services.

In a closely connected trend, we'll see increasing use of contextual information to improve security. Some of this context will be provided by the sensors built into devices, such as cameras and GPS receivers. In addition, analytical and monitoring tools will be able to gather valuable contextual information from the environment. For example, they may examine databases containing information about users' access history and other relevant data.

Baseline Security

A greater level of baseline, hardware-enforced security features will be important in all categories of device, from smartphones to full-featured PCs. These capabilities will protect the information on the device itself, and the information that is accessed from the device. They'll enable greater trust in the device, and because of this trust we'll be able to provide users of the device with access to more resources, as I described in Chapter 7. The potential business benefits include increased user satisfaction and productivity.

I believe that these features will become particularly valuable as the Internet of Things takes shape. Many new, connected devices and objects won't be powerful enough to run traditional software security controls. Do I expect the computers that control my car or my home to run full intrusion prevention systems or antivirus suites? No. But I do believe that they should include protection that limits their functions to the desired purpose, reducing the risk that they could be successfully attacked and manipulated via wireless networks.

For enterprise security, these baseline hardware security capabilities will provide help in key focus areas, including threat management, ID and access management, data protection, and remote monitoring. Some expected baseline capabilities include protected environments, encryption, hardware acceleration, enhanced recovery, and integration with security software, as described next.

Protected Environments

Increasingly, hardware will provide protection for essential functions and data in the form of trusted layers and execution environments. I think of this approach as analogous, at the hardware level, to the way we're implementing network security zones within Intel's enterprise environment (as described in Chapter 7). The most valuable and critical functions receive the greatest protection, as well as increased monitoring and recovery capabilities.

Attackers have become increasingly adept at compromises using tools, such as rootkits, that operate at or below the operating system level—making them harder to detect and prevent by security applications. Implementing protection at the hardware level can help prevent compromise of firmware, operating systems, hypervisors, and other fundamental system components. Hardware-level protection can also help alert security professionals to attempted attacks and aid in system recovery.

Encryption

Many organizations already use disk encryption to protect data against loss or theft. But in a world where devices are always on and always connected, traditional software-based hard disk encryption is not sufficient. New capabilities will make encryption an even more pervasive technology used to protect information throughout its life—both when it is stored and when it is transmitted. Devices will include self-encrypting drives that maximize protection while minimizing the performance impact; encrypted input-output will help protect data during communications. Capabilities that currently exist in larger systems, such as total memory encryption, will become common in PCs and other end-user devices.

Hardware Acceleration

There's often a trade-off between security and performance. Controls, such as software-based encryption and malware scans, certainly help increase protection, but the performance impact can also increase frustration for users, to such an extent that some may avoid using the security features altogether. Accelerating functions in hardware can shift the balance in favor of security by decreasing the impact, both on users and on enterprise systems. For example, complex calculations required by standard encryption algorithms can be accelerated using hardware instructions rather than executed entirely in software.

Enhanced Recovery

As I've discussed in previous chapters, we must assume that compromise is inevitable, despite our best efforts to prevent it. As attacks become increasingly sophisticated, the ability to recover from compromises will become even more important. Future capabilities will help organizations recover from low-level attacks that target fundamental system components such as firmware or the BIOS. The system will be able to detect changes in these components, whether due to malicious attacks or accidental corruption. It will then be able to take steps to restore the components to a known good state, alerting users and the security team when necessary. Other anticipated recovery features include enhanced capabilities to revoke cryptographic keys to reduce the spread and impact of compromise.

Integration with Security Software and Other Applications

Existing security suites and other applications will continue to play valuable roles in detecting, preventing, and recovering from attacks. They will be able to provide an even greater level of protection when they are integrated with hardware-based security. This integration will enable software to more closely monitor the underlying hardware for attacks that might otherwise go undetected. For example, security software may use hardware features to detect symptoms, such as memory state changes, caused by specific types of attack. The software will then be able to take action to remove the threat.

Context-Aware Security

The theme of context awareness underlies many of the rich user experiences described in this chapter. Context awareness can also enhance security: the same sensors and analytical tools that help organizations create personalized experiences can also be used to mitigate risk.

In the home, TVs might be able to recognize when a child is watching, and show only appropriate channels. In supermarkets, cameras that are already used for physical security could help increase the efficiency of automated checkout stations. As I described, image recognition technology can determine a shopper's approximate age. By using this information, perhaps in conjunction with data from a scanned driver's license, the system could help avoid the need for cashiers to manually approve alcohol sales—leading to faster checkouts for consumers and reduced costs for stores.

The sensors in portable devices, such as mobile PCs and smartphones, may also be used to help protect against theft and unauthorized use. A simple case might utilize the device's camera, microphone, and GPS receiver to help authenticate you as the device's owner. If the user looks and sounds like you, and the PC is at your house, we have more confidence that the person using it is really the owner.

Additional technologies in portable devices, such as NFC, will allow more sophisticated examples of context-aware security. Devices will know when they're no longer in proximity of their owner, and may enter a protected state to prevent data loss. If your phone is near your laptop, we have greater confidence that you are the user trying to access the information on the laptop. When your phone moves away, the laptop deduces that you have moved away, too, and begins to armor itself by locking the screen. As you move progressively farther away, the laptop first goes into standby to save power, and then begins encrypting its contents for protection.

The GPS receiver in a portable device can also be used to geofence the device and the data it contains. If the receiver detects that a PC has moved outside a specific area, the device could alert the owner and the enterprise support team. The same capabilities could help protect data whose movement is restricted by specific geography-related requirements such as export controls. The device could detect when it's in a country subject to these controls, and encrypt the data it contains to protect it.

Cloud Security and Context Awareness

Cloud service providers recognize that many businesses have been reluctant to move critical data to external clouds due to security, regulatory, and privacy concerns. Suppliers have been working to add security capabilities designed to address these concerns. As they do so, we can expect more cloud services that are differentiated based on the level of trust they offer.

Suppliers might offer a "plain vanilla" cloud service for noncritical applications, along with a more expensive high-trust cloud service. Besides offering additional technical controls, secure clouds might include guarantees that the supplier will meet specific privacy and other data-protection regulatory requirements. This tiered strategy resembles the zoned approach to network security that we are implementing within Intel's private cloud as part of our new security architecture. Zones that host critical applications are protected by a variety of controls, ranging from network segmentation and hardened virtualization host servers to additional monitoring.

Within our private cloud, we are also moving toward using context awareness to improve security. I expect external clouds to adopt this approach as well, including the use of client-aware clouds in combination with cloud-aware clients.

A basic level of client awareness already exists in web-based services. Client browsers may warn you if you're being directed to a suspicious-looking site; web services recognize that you're using a smartphone.

In the future, client-aware cloud services will be able to tailor the access they provide based on the security capabilities of the client in order to mitigate risk. In our private cloud, a fully managed device that includes hardware-based enterprise security features and a full software security suite may get more access than an unsecured personal device. At the same time, a cloud-aware client will be able to validate that the cloud service it is accessing is genuine, and that it offers the required level of security.

As businesses use a growing number of cloud services, security requirements become more complex. A single enterprise may use multiple external cloud services while also operating a private cloud and a traditional computing environment. It will be important to streamline access for users. We can expect more emphasis on technology that eliminates the need for users to authenticate to each individual service.

Business Intelligence and Data Protection

Security context can be provided not only by sensors, but also by analyzing information about the enterprise environment and the threat landscape. As attackers become stealthier, this analysis will become an increasingly important part of an organization's defenses. Within Intel, we are moving toward the use of business intelligence tools to analyze patterns of network traffic and system use. I expect to see increasingly sophisticated external services that analyze a broad range of information in order to detect and prevent attacks.

As information is used on more devices outside the enterprise network perimeter, it will also be increasingly important to focus on controls that are integrated with the data itself. Many organizations, including Intel, are already protecting information with technologies such as enterprise rights management. In the future, these capabilities are likely to become more sophisticated and automated, allowing businesses to define policies that automatically store sensitive data in highly secured locations.

Conclusion: The Implications for CISOs

New technologies bring challenges, but they also bring opportunities for the CISO and for the organization overall.

The rich context-aware experiences that I've described in this chapter are entirely dependent on IT. To deliver these experiences, organizations will need to understand and manage the risks. As the experts in information risk, CISOs and other security professionals should have opportunities to become closely involved in the development and implementation of key business initiatives. This will result in a higher profile for the information risk and security team across the entire organization.

To fully take advantage of these opportunities, CISOs will need broad business and people skills as well as a thorough knowledge of security controls. I'll discuss these skills further in the next chapter.

CHAPTER 9

The 21st Century CISO

The conductor of the orchestra doesn't make a sound. His power comes from awakening possibility in others.

—Benjamin Zander, conductor and coauthor of *The Art of Possibility*

The finance director sounded frustrated and exhausted. Our IT auditors had been trying to tell her about an obscure yet important data backup problem that affected SOX compliance. But her background was in accounting, not technology, and as the IT experts presented page after page of technical information elaborating the intricacies of backup processes, her eyes glazed over. The more they tried to explain by adding yet another layer of detail, the more confused and frustrated she became.

That's when I thought of a solution. "Imagine," I said, "we've got a passenger train running from station A to station B. That's what our backups are like; they're carrying data from our servers to tape."

"We know the train arrived at station B, so we know the backup occurred," I said. "But we don't know how many passengers got on at station A, and we don't know how many got off at station B. So we can't definitively say we actually backed up all the information, and to comply with SOX, we need to be certain."

The finance director sat up. For the first time since the start of the presentation, she seemed alert and engaged. And from that point on, we made progress. She asked how we planned to solve the problem, we briefly mentioned a couple of the possible solutions, and the meeting ended on an upbeat note.

My storytelling—using an off-the-cuff metaphor—succeeded where the more traditional approach had failed. It communicated a technical security issue in terms that a senior businessperson could understand and remember. And it illustrates one of the key skills of the 21st century CISO. We need to extend our reach outside the security organization to communicate with and influence people at all levels, from all backgrounds.

Chief Information Risk Officer

In this final chapter, I'll explain some of the skills and traits I believe CISOs need to fulfill their changing role. To set the stage, I'd like to step back for a moment and briefly recap the changing focus of information security overall.

Because information technology now supports every aspect of the business, the information risk and security group must also expand its scope to span the full breadth of information-related business risks, as described in Chapter 1. At many organizations, this is already happening. CISOs are taking on responsibility for privacy and regulatory compliance in addition to more traditional IT security functions.

This is a huge opportunity for CISOs to step into a more valuable, high-profile role within the organization. Perhaps the term *chief information risk officer* more accurately describes this role since it implies responsibility for the broad range of business and technology-related risks. The core skills of information security professionals—evaluating and mitigating risk—are as essential for mitigating new risks associated with privacy and regulatory compliance as they are for more traditional IT-related threats.

Taking on a larger role requires a broader view and a corresponding set of skills. We need to communicate in terms business people understand and build relationships that enable us to influence people at all levels across the organization. We also need extensive management and leadership skills, both to operate at an executive level and to inspire our security team.

The ability to manage the full range of information-related risks is a necessity, not just for the CISO, but for the organization. If we do not step into a broader role, the organization must acquire these abilities elsewhere. Because of this, CISOs who do not adapt to this role run the risk of becoming irrelevant to the organization.

I believe the 21st century CISO's broader skills are also the key to addressing one of the biggest continuing challenges facing security groups, which is obtaining funding for security initiatives. A few years ago, one CISO expressed his frustration this way: "Many CISOs have long expressed concern over their inability to obtain funding, to obtain resource and funding support for information security investments deemed necessary to provide suitable levels of protection." At conferences and meetings, I often ask other security professionals if they agree. Overwhelmingly, the answer is yes.

Funding security initiatives can undoubtedly be challenging for most organizations. But I also believe this quote is an indication of a failure within the security profession in general. This failure can be largely attributed to a lack of business acumen. Business acumen is necessary to communicate the technical risks in language nontechnical people in the business can grasp. It's also necessary to understand the perspective of others, including the fact that some risks are worth taking. Risk-taking is fundamental to business. Without it, no business value would be created.

The Z-Shaped Individual

If we don't already have the skills required of the 21st century CISO, we'll need to acquire them.

To some extent, this trend parallels what is happening in most technology-related professions: IT professionals need to acquire business acumen as well as depth of IT knowledge. The concept of "T-shaped" individuals has been widely used to describe the idea that IT professionals need to be able to provide value horizontally, across business groups in the organization, as well as vertically at all levels within IT.

This concept is useful, but it doesn't fully encompass the skills of the 21st century CISO. The unique role of CISOs and other security professionals might be better represented as a "Z-shaped" individual, as shown in Figure 9-1. Adding the third dimension of core security skills, such as risk assessment and understanding of controls, allows us to deliver value across the business and all areas of IT.

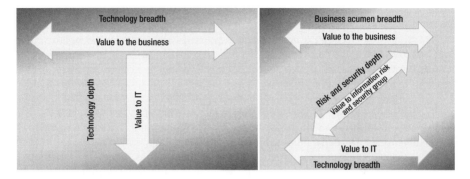

Figure 9-1. *The T-Shaped IT professional (left) and the Z-shaped CISO (right)*

The 21st century CISO needs to understand business priorities and processes well enough to identify how security controls help or constrain the business. To gain this level of understanding, he or she has probably gained experience in areas that are central to the company's business, which, of course, vary depending on the company's core focus. For example, the CISO might previously have worked in manufacturing operations, services, or mergers and acquisitions.

The CISO needs technical knowledge too, although the depth of technical knowledge required remains a subject of intense debate among my peers. I've observed CISOs at smaller and less-complex organizations who feel they need deeper technical skills to do their jobs. This is not surprising. With much smaller security teams, CISOs at smaller companies may need to be more involved in day-to-day technical details as well as managing people. At larger and more complex organizations, CISOs are less likely to spend time delving into technical detail.

However, all CISOs need to be able to understand enough about the technology to absorb the important issues and communicate these issues to other managers outside the security group. This means that our technical knowledge must be broad, ranging from devices to data centers. We need to know enough about devices, such as smartphones, PCs, and tablets, to understand the security implications as well as the benefits. At the other end of the scale, we need to know enough about data centers and physical access controls to understand and communicate the important security requirements and challenges.

Our core risk management and security skills provide the link that completes the "Z" by connecting technology and business. We understand how to assess and manage risk by applying procedural, technical, and physical controls to meet the organization's legal, privacy, and security requirements.

Foundational Skills

Becoming a Z-shaped individual is the foundation for one of the 21st century CISO's essential traits: establishing credibility across the organization. We must be credible in order to build trusted relationships with executives and specialists across the organization and to discuss the vast range of issues that affect the business. This credibility is built on the competence that comes from understanding the business and technology as well as possessing core security skills.

Our ability to influence the organization also springs from a clear mission. I use the term *centered* to describe this. We can effectively present our case because we have a strong sense of purpose and a clear understanding of why the security group exists and what we are trying to achieve.

This idea returns us to the theme of this book: Protect to Enable. In our global economy, Intel, like most companies, operates in highly competitive markets. As the security organization, our mission is to enable the free flow of information and rapid implementation of new capabilities to ensure success and long-term competitive survival. Other CISOs may work at more risk-averse organizations, and therefore some aspects of their mission may differ from ours. However, the mission is always aligned with the business priorities, and it becomes an essential part of who we are. It provides a sense of purpose that lends authenticity and consistency to our actions and helps us build credibility across the organization.

As we all know, security can be a particularly distracting profession, with a constant barrage of day-to-day emergencies and diversions. So we need a clear mission in order to retain a strong sense of direction. Like expert sailors, we can progress toward our goal amid the day-to-day distractions and diversions, making continual adjustments and corrections to stay on course as the winds shift.

We also need to retain a sense of curiosity. To engage with others, we need to be genuinely interested in what they do. This curiosity enables us to continue to learn, building on and broadening the competencies that then enhance our credibility.

Another major reason we need to be learners is to stay ahead of the enemy. Threat agents are always learning because they must. As new threats emerge, we put in place new controls. But once implemented, these controls tend to be static, while threat agents are dynamic, coming up with new techniques to bypass the controls. Therefore, our thinking must also be dynamic, and we must continually learn in order to protect against ever-evolving threats.

Becoming a Storyteller

We cannot influence people unless we communicate with them. And as the scope of information risk expands, we need to communicate with a wider range of people across the organization.

Communicating with people isn't always easy, as most of us have discovered. If we start relaying technology details to those who aren't technologists, we won't capture their interest. In fact, we run the risk of doing the opposite, as I described in the example at the start of this chapter.

To communicate, CISOs must become chameleon-like, with the ability to blend into a variety of environments. We need enough knowledge of each business domain to be able to communicate with different groups using language they understand. And we need to discuss these subjects at different levels. A CFO may only want to hear a high-level summary expressed in terms of financial impact and return, which is often not easy when discussing security investments targeting hard-to-quantify threats. Product group managers want to hear security issues expressed in terms that relate to sales, marketing, and operational efficiency.

I've found storytelling to be a powerful tool for communicating with diverse people across the organization. When I frame security issues as stories and images that people can understand, they relate better to the issues even if they lack a background in technology.

I like to tell stories using metaphors and analogies. They are easily remembered, and they translate complex subjects into simple terms everyone can understand. In fact, the metaphors I've used throughout this book, such as the perfect storm in Chapter 1, the train backup in this chapter, and the roundabouts and traffic lights in Chapter 5, have helped me communicate security issues to many people both within and outside Intel.

To paraphrase Benjamin Zander, the conductor and visionary, the power of an orchestra's conductor comes from awakening possibility in others (Zander and Zander 2000). In the same way, I believe the power of the CISO comes from awakening the awareness of risk among people across the organization. I use stories based on metaphors to create that awareness.

For example, employees often find it hard to understand the dangers of stealthy threats. This is because the threats are unobtrusive, concealing themselves so they can steal information over the long term. Users are usually not even aware that a problem exists on their system. They still associate malware with obvious, annoying symptoms such as screen messages and system crashes. So when we tell them we've detected dangerous software on their machine, they have a hard time believing that it matters.

To communicate the danger, I sometimes use the analogy of ants and termites. "Malware used to be like food-eating ants in the kitchen," I explain. "You'd know when you had an infestation because you'd see ants crawling over the countertops and walls. Once you knew about them, you'd spray or set traps to eliminate them.

"But today, threats are more like the termites that can live in your walls. You can't see them, and you may not even know they are there. But they're doing much more damage than ants ever did. In fact, they may be destroying the structural integrity of your house."

I've found using analogies helps quickly drive home messages. People immediately understand that these invisible threats can undermine the structure of the computing environment, just as termites undermine houses. This makes them more likely to accept the next step, which is that we have to perform the digital equivalent of tenting their computer to eradicate the vermin.

Fear Is Junk Food

Just as building trusted relationships is essential to influencing the organization, I also think we need to transcend the doom-and-gloom that can pervade discussions of security topics.

The security industry has a tendency to use fear to sell products. Internally, as security professionals, we sometimes share this tendency. Of course, security really is about scary things: threats, vulnerabilities, and risk. But focusing on fear as the primary motivator is like living on a diet of junk food. It may provide immediate gratification, and it's somewhat addictive, but ultimately it's not healthy for either the CISO or the rest of the organization.

In the short term, fear can scare people into action and help drive funding for security projects. However, relying on fear alone can only work for so long. Eventually, it has the opposite effect. It causes the CISO to lose credibility. In fact, I think relying on fear may even contribute to the high rate of job turnover among CISOs. Those who rely too much on selling fear are snacking on an unhealthy diet, and eventually the organization realizes this and rejects them.

Ultimately, fear doesn't work for other reasons too. Most people don't want to listen to a continuous stream of negativity. If we are always seen as the source of negativity, we will lose our audience. If we are continually viewed as the group that says no, we will be ignored. People will bypass security restrictions in order to meet their business needs.

Even within the security organization, fear can become a gravitational force—a black hole—drawing ever-increasing attention to the negative side of security issues and draining energy that should be directed to enabling the business.

Accentuating the Positive

So how do we take a more positive approach? We must focus on our mission—Protect to Enable. This mission shifts the emphasis from the negative to the positive: how we can help the business achieve its goals by solving security problems. It puts hope and optimism before the challenge.

This mission is aligned with the business. Rather than being antagonistic, it is based on common values. It sets an optimistic tone, and, in the long term, optimism is a far better motivator than pessimism. Threats may be frightening, but our goal is to see past the threats and identify the opportunities. To paraphrase the noted Stanford University behavioral scientist Chip Heath, there's no problem that cannot be solved without a new framework. Therefore, if we can't see a solution, we have the wrong framework. Protect to Enable provides this new framework. It helps us focus on finding solutions.

Imagine you're invited to attend a meeting to discuss whether the company should start using a specific cloud-based business application from a new supplier. Clearly, this product introduces risks: it comes from an unfamiliar supplier, it's accessed over the Internet, and it means sensitive data will be stored outside the enterprise.

A narrow security view might focus solely on minimizing the risk. However, this narrow view can lead to a Catch-22 situation, as discussed in Clayton Christensen's book *The Innovator's Dilemma* (Harvard Business School Press, 1997). Typically, it goes something like this. To minimize the risk, the organization initially restricts the use of a new technology. For example, the technology can only be used for low-risk data, or by a narrow segment of employees. The problem with this approach is that it also reduces the business benefit to the point that the benefit of the technology cannot justify the expense and effort of adopting it. So we reach an impasse. To make the technology a viable proposition, we need to be able to show a business benefit—but we can't show a business benefit because we won't allow viable use of the technology.

Protect to Enable provides the new framework that frees us from the innovator's dilemma. It allows us to focus on the opportunity and identify benefits that outweigh the risks. For example, introducing a new supplier increases competition for our existing suppliers—leading to future savings for our organization. This benefit aligns with the business and is one that everyone in the organization understands. Perhaps less intuitive, but equally important, the savings can be used to fund security controls to mitigate the risk of using the technology more widely. Now our benefit/risk equation has a positive result rather than a negative one. By enabling the technology to be used more widely, we realize bigger business benefits that outweigh the additional cost of controls. This example also underlines the need for CISOs to build business acumen that enables us to see the opportunity and how it can be used to overcome the challenge of funding security initiatives.

Let's look at another example, this time from our experience at Intel in the days before we had defined our Protect to Enable mission. Several years ago, a highly damaging worm was discovered in our environment, requiring a significant emergency response from our team. Upon investigating, we traced the origin of the worm to an employee's personal computer.

Our immediate response was that of a stereotypical security group. We shut down this usage to eliminate the risk of future infections. We immediately tightened security policy to ensure only Intel-owned PCs could access the network, and we ruthlessly went through the environment and cut off access by any devices not managed by IT.

Our response was successful in the sense that it reduced the risk of infection. But it led to other risks we hadn't foreseen. Eliminating personally owned PCs from the network meant we now needed to issue corporate PCs to contract employees. This meant that we had to provide more people with devices that allowed full access to the Intel environment. It also, of course, increased capital costs. The broader impact was that it eliminated the potential business benefits of letting people use their own personal devices for work.

More recently—driven largely by employee demand, as well as the massive proliferation of new consumer devices—we revisited this issue. This time, we examined it from the perspective of Protect to Enable. We looked at the business opportunities if we allowed personally owned systems on the network, and then how we could mitigate the risks. As I mentioned in Chapter 1, we rapidly discovered that the business value is enormous. Helping employees communicate and collaborate at any time can drive significant productivity gains. It also helps make employees happy. They love using their personal smartphones, PCs, and tablets and appreciate that we enable them to do so.

These benefits easily outweigh the cost of the technology required to reduce the risk of allowing access by personal devices. True, some of this technology wasn't available at the time we experienced the original security problem. But if we had focused on the opportunity first, perhaps we could have found ways to provide some level of access while mitigating the risk, and experienced at least some of the benefits we enjoy today.

Demonstrating the Reality of Risk

Of course, the security organizations' role still centers on managing risk, which includes discussing the negative consequences of people's actions. If we frame this discussion carefully, I believe we can inform without fearmongering. By describing possible outcomes and solutions without using emotional language, in terms listeners can understand, we create a context in which the organization can make the decisions that are best for the business.

MEASURING AND COMMUNICATING THE VALUE OF SECURITY INVESTMENTS

Analyzing and communicating the value of security controls often presents challenges, particularly when it comes to expressing this value in terms that business people can understand.

This situation can be frustrating for security professionals, finance specialists, and business groups. Adding to the challenges, security investment decisions have become more complex as we analyze new options to counter threats, such as social engineering, and to support technology trends such as IT consumerization.

We created a security investment model designed to address these issues by helping us analyze investments based on their business value to Intel (Carty, Pimont, and Schmid 2012). The most important output of our model is an estimated financial value for each investment, based on how much the investment reduces risk. The spreadsheet-based model presents this information in a format easily understood by business professionals.

A key strength of our model is that we can analyze the value of each investment within the context of our IT environment, rather than in isolation. For example, we can estimate the incremental value that a new investment will provide when added to our existing controls. In addition, we can use the model to analyze any type of new or existing security investment.

We are already using the model to help drive discussions within Intel IT and more broadly across Intel. We have used the model to analyze new security initiatives and examine existing controls to identify areas where we may need to adjust our strategy.

Even when we have to highlight unpleasant outcomes, we're not fearmongering if our information is based clearly on reality. Here's another example from our experiences at Intel. As our customers' use of the Internet expanded, Intel's marketing groups naturally wanted to expand their external online presence by creating new web sites. So we, as Intel's information security group, began assessing the risks and the security controls required. Some of our marketing teams didn't find this an appealing prospect. They needed to move quickly, with the freedom to communicate however they thought best, and they viewed security procedures as bureaucracy that slowed them down and hindered their ability to communicate with customers and partners.

What happened next was far more persuasive than any of our initial efforts to forestall potential problems. A few web sites were launched without rigorous quality control. Hackers found the weaknesses in these sites, but they didn't crash the sites or steal information. Instead, they inserted links to porn sites.

When this unfortunate fact was discovered, it provided the leverage we needed to improve security procedures. I realized this was a case where a picture spoke a thousand words. So, to illustrate the impact, I simply showed the links to people within Intel. This wasn't fearmongering. It was simply demonstrating the real consequences of their actions on the Intel brand. Everyone could understand the implied question: Do we want our brand to look like this? This ended, once and for all, any discussion about whether we needed to apply rigorous quality control to external web sites.

The CISO's Sixth Sense

In the book *Blink: The Power of Thinking Without Thinking*, author Malcolm Gladwell (Little, Brown & Co., 2005) describes an interesting experiment. Researchers asked subjects to play a game in which they could maximize their winnings by turning over cards from either of two decks. What the subjects didn't know was that the decks were subtly stacked. They could win by selecting from one of the decks, but selecting from the other deck would ultimately lead to disaster. After about 80 cards, the subjects could explain the difference between the decks. But they had a hunch something was wrong much sooner, after only 50 cards. And they began showing signs of stress and changing their behavior even sooner, after only about 10 cards, long before they cognitively understood a difference existed.

As CISOs, we develop a sixth sense about security issues. Often, my instincts suggest a need to act or begin investigating a specific direction long before our group is able to fully understand or explain what is happening. This sixth sense is particularly relevant in the security realm, where our information is almost always imperfect or incomplete. When a threat strikes, we do not have time to conduct extensive research or wait for evidence to accumulate. Therefore, we need to act decisively based on imperfect information.

I think we develop this sixth sense from the diverse experiences and skills we've acquired during our careers. We can also foster this sixth sense by being aware. Some security professionals tend to be inwardly focused, looking only at the data and systems they need to protect. As described in Chapter 4, at Intel we try to be more open and outward-looking, sharing information, and seeking input from a variety of sources, including peers across our company and at other organizations. This can help CISOs spot early warning signals and correlate information to quickly identify threats. Like secret service agents scanning a crowd, our experience helps us spot anomalies, to see the signals and ignore the noise.

By intercepting threats early, we may be able to minimize or entirely eliminate the impact. We may also reduce the effort needed to deal with the threat. Early action may avoid the need for emergency response and a potentially major cleanup effort.

Taking Action at the Speed of Trust

A sixth sense is only of value if the organization can act on it quickly. This requires two things. First, we need the courage to take a leap of faith based on what we believe. This courage is rooted in the attributes I discussed earlier in this chapter, such as being centered and credible, with a clear sense of our mission.

The second requirement is that the organization responds quickly when we inform them about a security issue. This rapid response is only possible if we have established trusted relationships with people across the organization. Because of these relationships, the organization can act at the *Speed of Trust*, as Stephen M. R. Covey describes it in the book of the same name (Free Press, 2008). Faster, frictionless decisions are possible because people know, from experience, that our information is reliable and that our focus is on enabling rather than spreading fear.

The CISO As a Leader

Above all, 21st century CISOs must become effective leaders who can inspire their teams to enable and protect the organization.

Over the years, I've identified three essential themes I try to instill in my team and constantly reinforce in our day-to-day interactions. Our security team members must believe in our mission; feel they belong to our Intel IT security group and Intel as a whole; and feel they matter.

If I can make people feel they believe, they belong, and they matter, they will tackle any challenge. If people understand the greater goal, it helps establish an emotional connection and guide their everyday actions. This is a key reason that I have thought so much about defining our mission, and that I spend so much time helping our team see how their jobs are connected to the business's objectives and concerns.

For example, a typical operational goal might be to patch all systems within a week of a new software release. This goal is more meaningful if we establish the links to the business using I believe, I belong, and I matter. I believe in the mission of Protect to Enable. If I'm not protecting to enable, the other employees at the organization I belong to cannot do their jobs effectively. The company doesn't achieve its results, and the company doesn't execute its vision. Patching systems quickly matters because it helps our users do their jobs, which in turn helps the business achieve its goals.

Learning from Other Business Leaders

As leaders, we can learn a lot from how other business leaders work. Today, managers are moving away from command-and-control to a more collaborative approach that takes advantage of the diversity of employee ideas and strengths. I'm not talking about a consensus process, which can lead to endless debate and indecision. Rather, a leader's goal is to ensure alignment to a common mission and accelerate decisions. Within this framework, differing viewpoints and debate spark creativity, generating new ideas and a productive tension that can drive results.

Because security can be frustrating, even daunting, it's vital to find ways to help employees stay motivated. It's important to help employees feel they are making progress, not just when they achieve major milestones, but in solving the smaller problems they face every day. A key study found that even small wins boost motivation, productivity, and creativity. In the *Harvard Business Review* article describing the study, authors Teresa Amabile and Steven Kramer (2011) determined that the feeling of making progress is the most important contributor to an employee's emotions, motivations, and perceptions.

Opportunities to lead occur continually, in every interaction with our teams, with other people in IT, and with business partners. The question we need to ask ourselves is whether we are seizing these opportunities to reinforce our mission, and ultimately to help the organization achieve success.

In highly technical jobs and organizations, we have a tendency to focus on technical challenges while overlooking the "people factor." I think it's important to remember the need for personal connections, which foster the sense of belonging. When we know a little more about each other, we care more as a result. I think about this in my day-to-day interactions. If a team member is making a presentation, are we paying attention and asking thought-provoking questions, or are we distracted? And if so, do we think they will feel they belong?

When we meet with a team member to discuss their struggles with a project, are we helping them think through the issues and come up with solutions? Are we helping them believe they can overcome the challenges and that the results will matter to the company and to us? Or are we just taking them to task? Each interaction is an opportunity for coaching and helping employees improve their performance.

It goes without saying that leadership means taking responsibility. Yet some CISOs seem to forget this, at least occasionally. A typical situation goes something like this. The CISO warned of a security issue but couldn't obtain the budget or resources to address it. So the CISO abdicated responsibility because someone else had made the decision not to fund a solution. I take a different view. I believe even if we disagree with the decision, we should do our best. As partners in the organization's strategy, we should commit to the decision and share full accountability and responsibility with our peers.

A final requirement of effective leadership is the ability to develop other leaders within the security group. Otherwise, the group's strengths in managing risk for the business will last only as long as the current CISO's tenure. By building competence in depth, the CISO can ensure that the organization delivers sustained performance over time.

Looking to the Future

As the technology environment continues to evolve, many people believe we're moving toward a future in which organizations outsource much of the delivery of IT services. If this trend continues, what does it mean for the CISO?

In this view of the future, the organization shifts away from IT implementation to procurement and management of suppliers and services, while setting direction and establishing an overall IT architecture.

In addition to this, the organization will need to retain the core competency of the security group, the management of information risk. Essentially, organizations cannot outsource risk. We can hire companies to deliver our business systems, but we're still responsible for compliance with SOX. And if a breach results in theft or leakage of personal information, we're still responsible for reporting it. Furthermore, we still suffer the damage to our brand, even if the breach was due a failure of the supplier's systems. As regulations proliferate and more and more personal information is stored in business systems, the risks can only increase.

Therefore the CISO's abilities will remain essential, even if the job title changes. The organization must retain the management of information risk as a core competency.

As CISOs, we are poised to continue providing that core competency as long as we can effectively work within this new environment by developing the abilities I've described in this chapter and throughout this book. These abilities enable us to work with others to support the Protect to Enable mission.

C-I-S-O ATTRIBUTES

In this chapter, I have covered a range of abilities and characteristics that the 21st century CISO requires. Many of these probably sound familiar, but it's all too easy to forget them amid the demands of hectic daily schedules. I've found a good way to remind myself of some of the key attributes is simply to look at my job title. The letters in CISO help me remember that we all need Character, Intuition, Skills, and Objectivity. So if you're struggling to remember all the details in this chapter, just remember you're a CISO. You need Character to ensure your actions demonstrate integrity; Intuition to anticipate what's needed and act accordingly, taking risks when necessary; Skills that span business, technology, and a wide variety of risk areas; and Objectivity in order to avoid falling prey to fearmongering.

CHAPTER 10

References

Accenture. 2012. *Accenture Technology Vision 2012*. http://www.accenture.com/us-en/technology/technology-labs/Pages/insight-accenture-technology-vision-2012.aspx.

Ahamad, Mustaque. 2011. *Georgia Tech Releases Cyber Threats Forecast for 2012*. Comment in Georgia Tech press release. http://www.scs.gatech.edu/content/georgia-tech-releases-cyber-threats-forecast-2012.

Alperovitch, Dmitri. 2012. Comment in *Georgia Tech Emerging Cyber Threats Report 2012*. http://www.gtisc.gatech.edu/doc/emerging_cyber_threats_report2012.pdf.

Amabile, Teresa M., and Steven J. Kramer. 2011. "The Power of Small Wins." *Harvard Business Review* 89:5.

Bazerman, Max H. and Ann E. Tenbrunsel. 2011. *Blind Spots: Why We Fail to Do What's Right and What to Do about It*. Princeton: Princeton University Press.

Ben-Shalom, Omer, Manish Dave, Toby Kohlenberg, Dennis Morgan, Stacy Purcell, Alan Ross, Timothy Verrall, and Tarun Viswanathan. 2011. "Rethinking Information Security to Improve Business Agility." Intel Corporation. http://www.intel.com/content/www/us/en/enterprise-security/intel-it-enterprise-security-rethinking-information-security-to-improve-business-agility-paper.html.

Breakwell, Glynis. 2007. *The Psychology of Risk*. Cambridge, UK: Cambridge University Press.

Brito, Jerry and Tate Watkins. 2012. "Loving the Cyber Bomb? The Dangers of Threat Inflation in Cybersecurity Policy." *Harvard Law School National Security Journal*, 3:39–83.

Buczek, Laurie and Malcolm Harkins. 2009. "Developing an Enterprise Social Computing Strategy." Intel Corporation. http://www.intel.com/content/www/us/en/enterprise-reliability/intel-it-developing-enterprise-social-computing-strategy-paper.html.

Carty, Matt, Vincent Pimont, and David W. Schmid. 2012. "Measuring the Value of Information Security Investments." Intel Corporation. http://www.intel.com/content/www/za/en/it-management/intel-it-best-practices/information-security-investments-paper.html.

Casey, Timothy. 2007. "Threat Agent Library Helps Identify Information Security Risks." Intel Corporation. http://www.intel.com/it/pdf/threat-agent-library.pdf.

Casey, Tim and Brian Willis. 2008. "Wargames: Serious Play that Tests Enterprise Security Assumptions." Intel Corporation. http://www.intel.com/it/pdf/Wargames-Serious_Play_that_Tests_Enterprise_Security_Assumptions.pdf.

Christensen, Clayton M. 1997. *The Innovator's Dilemma: When New Technologies Cause Great Firms to Fail*. Boston, Mass.: Harvard Business School Press.

Cisco Systems, Inc. 2011a. *Cisco Connected World Technology Report 2011.* http://www.cisco.com/en/US/netsol/ns1120/index.html.

Cisco Systems, Inc. 2011b. *Email Attacks: This Time It's Personal.* http://www.cisco.com/en/US/prod/collateral/vpndevc/ps10128/ps10339/ps10354/targeted_attacks.pdf.

Clark, Sandy, Stefan Frei, Matt Blaze, Jonathan Smith. 2010. "Familiarity Breeds Contempt: The Honeymoon Effect and the Role of Legacy Code in Zero-Day Vulnerabilities." In *Proceedings of the 26th Annual Computer Security Applications Conference.* New York: Association for Computing Machinery. doi: 10.1145/1920261.1920299.

Colgan, William B. 2010. *Allied Strafing in World War II: A Cockpit View of Air to Ground Battle.* Jefferson, NC: McFarland.

Corporate Executive Board Company, The (CEB). 2012. Information Risk Executive Council. Arlington, VA. http://www.executiveboard.com/exbd/information-technology/it-risk/index.page.

Covey, Stephen M. R. with Rebecca R. Merrill. 2008. *The Speed of Trust: The One Thing That Changes Everything.* New York: Free Press.

CSO Magazine, US Secret Service, Software Engineering Institute CERT Program at Carnegie Mellon University, Deloitte. 2011. *2011 CyberSecurity Watch Survey: Organizations Need More Skilled Cyber Professionals To Stay Secure.* Press release. http://www.sei.cmu.edu/newsitems/cybersecurity_watch_survey_2011.cfm.

Culp, Scott. 2010. *10 Immutable Laws of Security.* Microsoft Corporation. http://technet.microsoft.com/library/cc722487.aspx.

CWE/SANS. 2011. *CWE/SANS TOP 25 Most Dangerous Software Errors.* http://cwe.mitre.org/top25/.

Department of Telecommunications, Government of India. 2009. Instructions to Internet service providers. Letter dated February 23, 2009, No. 820-1/2008-DS Pt. II.

Edwards, Cliff, Olga Kharif, and Michael Riley. 2011. "Human Errors Fuel Hacking as Test Shows Nothing Stops Idiocy." Bloomberg News. Posted June 27, 2011. http://www.bloomberg.com/news/2011-06-27/human-errors-fuel-hacking-as-test-shows-nothing-prevents-idiocy.html.

European Commission. 2011. *ePrivacy Directive: circumstances, procedures and formats for personal data breach notifications.* http://ec.europa.eu/information_society/policy/ecomm/doc/library/public_consult/data_breach/ePrivacy_databreach_consultation.pdf.

European Commission. 2012. *Proposal for a regulation of the European Parliament and of the Council on the protection of individuals with regard to the processing of personal data and on the free movement of such data* (*General Data Protection Regulation*). http://ec.europa.eu/justice/data-protection/document/review2012/com_2012_11_en.pdf.

European Network and Information Security Agency (ENISA). 2010. *Incentives and Challenges for Information Sharing in the Context of Network and Information Security.* http://www.enisa.europa.eu/activities/Resilience-and-CIIP/public-private-partnership/information-sharing-exchange/incentives-and-barriers-to-information-sharing.

Evered, Rob and Jerzy Rub. 2010. "Maintaining Information Security while Allowing Personal Hand-held Devices in the Enterprise." Intel Corporation. http://www.intel.com/content/www/us/en/enterprise-security/intel-it-enterprise-security-maintaining-information-security-while-allowing-personal-handheld-devices-paper.html.

Fleming, Virgil and Naoyuki Tomizawa. 2012. "Intel IT: Keeping the Business Running in a Crisis." Intel Corporation. http://www.intel.com/content/www/us/en/it-management/intel-it-best-practices/intel-it-keeping-business-running-in-crisis.html.

Fong, David, Toby Kohlenberg, and Justin Philips. 2010. "Enterprise Security Benefits of Microsoft Windows 7." Intel Corporation. http://www.intel.com/content/www/us/en/windows-7-upgrade/intel-it-windows-7-upgrade-security-brief.html.

Gartner, Inc. 2005. *Gartner Survey Shows Spending for Compliance and Corporate Governance to Account for 10–15 Percent of an Enterprise's 2006 IT Budget.* Gartner Inc. Press release. http://www.gartner.com/press_releases/asset_141532_11.html.

Gartner, Inc. 2011a. *Gartner Says Context-Aware Technologies Will Affect $96 Billion of Annual Consumer Spending Worldwide by 2015.* Gartner Inc. Press release. http://www.gartner.com/it/page.jsp?id=1827614.

Gartner, Inc. 2011b. *Gartner Identifies the Top 10 Strategic Technologies for 2012.* Gartner Inc. Press release. http://www.gartner.com/it/page.jsp?id=1826214.

Etherington, Darrell. 2012. "Apple envisions a future where clothes inform and mold your workouts." *GigaOm.* Posted Jan 17, 2012. http://gigaom.com/apple/apple-envisions-a-future-where-clothes-inform-and-mold-your-workouts/.

Gladwell, Malcolm. 2005. *Blink: The Power of Thinking Without Thinking.* New York: Little, Brown & Co.

Gutierrez, Esteban, Toby Kohlenberg, Sridhar Mahankali, and Bill Sunderland. 2012. "Virtualizing High-security Servers in a Private Cloud." Intel Corporation. http://www.intel.com/content/www/us/en/it-management/intel-it-best-practices/cloud-security-and-secure-virtualization-paper.html.

Henry Ford Museum, The. 2003. "The Life of Henry Ford." http://www.hfmgv.org/exhibits/hf/.

Information Risk Executive Council. 2011. *Security Controls Maturity Benchmark Summary.* Information published in *2011–2012 Intel IT Performance Report.* Intel Corporation. http://www.intel.com/content/www/us/en/it-management/intel-it-best-practices/intel-it-annual-performance-report-2011-12.html.

Intel Corporation. 2010. Form 10-Q for the quarterly period ended March 27, 2010; Filed May 3, 2010. http://www.intc.com/secfiling.cfm?filingID=950123-10-42822.

Intel Corporation. 2011. *Worldwide Device Estimates Year 2020—Intel One Smart Network Work.*

Intel Corporation. 2012a. "Thinking Differently About IT Value: 2011–2012 Intel IT Performance Report." http://www.intel.com/content/www/us/en/it-management/intel-it-best-practices/intel-it-annual-performance-report-2011-12.html.

Intel Corporation. 2012b. "Intel Works with HSN, Kraft Foods and Macy's to Transform the Shopping Experience." Intel Corporation press release, January 15, 2012. http://newsroom.intel.com/community/intel_newsroom/blog/2012/01/15/intel-works-with-hsn-kraft-foods-and-macys-to-transform-the-shopping-experience.

Jackson Higgins, Kelly. 2010. "'Operation Aurora' Changing the Role of the CISO." *Dark Reading* March 16, 2010. http://www.darkreading.com/database-security/167901020/security/attacks-breaches/223900131/operation-aurora-changing-the-role-of-the-ciso.html.

Joffe-Walt, Chana and Alix Spiegel. 2012. "Psychology Of Fraud: Why Good People Do Bad Things." National Public Radio broadcast. Transcript accessed online May 28, 2012. http://www.npr.org/2012/05/01/151764534/psychology-of-fraud-why-good-people-do-bad-things.

Johnson, Steven. 2010. *Where Good Ideas Come From: The Natural History of Innovation.* New York: Riverhead Books, a subsidiary of Penguin Books (USA).

Johnson, Steven. 2010. Talk at TEDGlobal 2010. http://www.ted.com/talks/steven_johnson_where_good_ideas_come_from.html.

Keteyian, Armen. 2010. "Digital Photocopiers Loaded With Secrets." CBS News article posted online April 20, 2010. http://www.cbsnews.com/2100-18563_162-6412439.html.

Leon, Fred. 2011. "Securing Intel's External Online Presence." Intel Corporation. http://www.intel.com/content/www/us/en/enterprise-security/intel-it-securing-intels-external-online-presence-paper.html.

Levin, Carl. 2010. Opening Statement of Senator Carl Levin, Senate Armed Services Committee Hearing on Nominations of Vice Admiral James A. Winnefeld and Lieutenant General Keith B. Alexander.

Lindstrom, Pete. 2008. "Five Immutable Laws of Virtualization Security." Burton Group blog entry posted online January 08, 2008. http://srmsblog.burtongroup.com/2008/01/five-immutable.html.

LosHuertos, Gary. 2010. "Herding Firesheep in New York City" Blog entry posted online October 27, 2010. http://technologysufficientlyadvanced.blogspot.com/2010/10/herding-firesheep-in-new-york-city.html.

Massachusetts Institute of Technology Sloan School Center for Information Systems Research. 2012. IT Governance. http://cisr.mit.edu/research/research-overview/classic-topics/it-governance/.

McAfee, Inc. 2011. Press release. *McAfee Q2 2011 Threats Report Shows Significant Growth for Malware on Mobile Platforms.* http://www.mcafee.com/us/about/news/2011/q3/20110823-01.aspx.

Miller, Ron and Joe Varga. 2011. "Benefits of Enabling Personal Handheld Devices in the Enterprise." http://www.intel.com/content/www/us/en/intel-innovation/inte-it-it-leadership-benefits-of-enabling-personal-handheld-devices-in-the-enterprise-practices.html.

Nest Labs. 2012. Nest Learning Thermostat web site. http://www.nest.com/.

Perlroth, Nicole. 2011. "Insurance Against Cyber Attacks Expected to Boom." *New York Times* blog post December 29, 2011. http://bits.blogs.nytimes.com/2011/12/23/insurance-against-cyber-attacks-expected-to-boom/.

Rajab, Moheeb Abu, Lucas Ballard, Panayiotis Marvrommatis, Niels Provos, and Xin Zhao. 2010. "The Nocebo Effect on the Web: An Analysis of Fake Anti-Virus Distribution." In *Large-Scale Exploits and Emergent Threats.* Usenix. http://static.googleusercontent.com/external_content/untrusted_dlcp/research.google.com/en/us/pubs/archive/36346.pdf.

Rice, David. 2007. *Geekonomics: The Real Cost of Insecure Software.* Boston: Addison-Wesley Professional.

Seidman, Dov. 2011. "Measuring HOW We Do Business." *Forbes* article posted online November 27, 2011. http://www.forbes.com/sites/dovseidman/2011/11/27/measuring-how-we-do-business/.

Sinek, Simon. 2009. *Start with Why: How Great Leaders Inspire Everyone to Take Action.* New York: Portfolio.

Slovic, Paul. 2010. *The Feeling of Risk: New Perspectives on Risk Perception.* New York: Routledge.

Sunderland, Bill and Ajay Chandramouly. 2011. "Overcoming Security Challenges to Virtualize Internet-facing Applications." Intel Corporation. `http://www.intel.com/content/www/us/en/it-management/intel-it-best-practices/cloud-security-and-secure-virtualization-paper.html`.

Taleb, Nassim Nicholas. 2007. *The Black Swan: The Impact of the Highly Improbable*. New York: Random House.

Thaler, Richard H. Thaler and Cass R. Sunstein. 2008. *Nudge: Improving Decisions About Health, Wealth, and Happiness*. New Haven, CT: Yale University Press.

US Environmental Protection Agency (EPA). 2011. "Oil Pollution Act Overview." `http://www.epa.gov/oem/content/lawsregs/opaover.htm`.

US Government Accountability Office (GAO). 2012. "Challenges in Securing the Modernized Electricity Grid." `http://www.gao.gov/products/GAO-12-507T`.

US Securities and Exchange Commission. 2011. CF Disclosure Guidance: Topic No. 2. Issued October 13, 2011. `http://www.sec.gov/divisions/corpfin/guidance/cfguidance-topic2.htm`.

Van Derbeken, Jaxon. "S.F. officials locked out of computer network." *San Francisco Chronicle*. Published online Tuesday, July 15, 2008. `http://www.sfgate.com/bayarea/article/S-F-officials-locked-out-of-computer-network-3205200.php`.

Venables, Philip. 2008. Speech at RSA Conference 2008.

Verizon. 2011. *2011 Data Breach Investigations Report*. `http://www.verizonbusiness.com/resources/reports/rp_data-breach-investigations-report-2011_en_xg.pdf`.

Weil, Peter and Jeanne W. Ross. 2004. *IT Governance: How Top Performers Manage IT Decision Rights for Superior Results*. Boston, Mass.: Harvard Business School Press.

Willis, Brian. 2012. "Sharing Cyber-Threat Information: An Outcomes-based Approach." Intel Corporation. `http://www.intel.com/content/www/us/en/it-management/intel-it-best-practices/sharing-cyber-threat-information-an-outcomes-based-approach.html`.

Zander, Rosamund Stone and Benjamin Zander. 2000. *The Art of Possibility: Transforming Professional and Personal Life*. Boston, Mass.: Harvard Business School Press.

Index